101 SPOOKTACULAR PARTY IDEAS

Fun Halloween Recipes, Games, Decorations and Craft Ideas For Ghosts and Ghouls Of All Ages

Linda Sadler

First Edition

Creative **Kids** Products

Kansas City, Missouri

101 Spooktacular Party Ideas

Fun Halloween Recipes, Games, Decorations and Craft Ideas For Ghosts and Ghouls Of All Ages

By Linda Sadler

Published By: Creative Kids Products
9825 NE 116th St
Kansas City, MO 64157-1106   U.S.A.

Printed in the United States of America

ISBN 0-9658527-6-8

Publisher's Cataloging-in-Publication
(Provided by Quality Books, Inc.)

Sadler, Linda.
    101 spooktacular party ideas : fun Halloween recipes, games, decorations and craft ideas for ghosts and ghouls of all ages / Linda Sadler. -- 1st ed.
        p. cm.
        LCCN: 00-190596
        ISBN: 0-9658527-6-8

    1. Halloween decorations. 2. Halloween cookery. 3. Entertaining. 4. Games. I. Title.

TT900.H32.S23 2000   745.594'1
                            QBI00-368

TABLE OF CONTENTS

INTRODUCTION... 5
HELPFUL SUGGESTIONS.. 6

SPOOKTACULAR OUTDOOR DECORATIONS
1. Haunted Graveyard—Picket Fence............................ 10
2. Haunted Graveyard—Tombstones............................ 11
3. Haunted Graveyard—Fresh Gravesites 12
4. Halloween Luminaries 12
5. Headless Ghoul 13
6. Monster Footprints... 14
7. Sinister Yard Signs 15
8. Flying Ghosts 16
9. Humongous Spiders 17

SPOOKTACULAR INDOOR DECORATIONS
10. Creepy Signs 20
11. Friendly Ghosts 21
12. Flying Bats 22
13. Streamers.. 24
14. Open If You Dare Box 25
15. Disembodied Heads 26
16. Haunted Tunnel.. 27
17. Candy Corn Candles 28
18. Spooktacular Lighting..................................... 29
19. Small Touches 31

QUICK & EASY SPOOKTACULAR TREATS
20. Cool Eyeballs.. 34
21. Dirt Cups.. 35
22. Bugs On A Log 36
23. Caramel Apples.. 37
24. Spider Treats 38
25. Witches Hats 39

QUICK & EASY SPOOKTACULAR TREATS (CONTINUED)

26. Goblins Nutty Mix 39
27. Graveyard Ghosts.. 40
28. Spooktacular Fruit Pizza 41
29. Monster Crunch 42

MAKE AHEAD SPOOKTACULAR TREATS

30. Cheesy Eyeballs 44
31. Deviled Eyeballs 45
32. Spicy Bat Wings & Boo Cheese Dip 46
33. Halloween Sandwiches 48
34. All Hallows Eve Dip 49
35. Toasted Bones 50
36. Roasted Pumpkin Seeds 51
37. Devils Snack Mix... 52
38. Halloween Popcorn Balls.. 53
39. Ooey Gooey Wormy Dessert 54
40. Spider's Ice Scream Pie 55
41. Mini Ghost Cookies 56
42. Ice Scream Sandwiches.. 57
43. Slithering Dessert... 58
44. Spider Web Brownies 59

SPOOKTACULAR BREWS AND OTHER IDEAS

45. Witches Brew... 62
46. Vampire Blood Smoothies 63
47. Kiddie Brew 64
48. Vampire Punch.. 65
49. Black Magic Punch 66
50. Boil & Bubble Brew 67
51. Pumpkin Punch Bowl 68
52. Spooktacular Ice Cubes... 68
53. Boiling Caldron.. 69
54. Frozen Zombie Hands.. 70

Spooktacular Relay Games

55. Pass The Pumpkin 72
56. Follow The Ghost Relay............................... 73
57. Eyeball Dig Relay 74
58. Evil Twin Relay... 76
59. Witch Drawing Relay 78
60. Winter Costume Relay 79
61. Suck It Up Relay 80
62. Pass The Kiss Relay 81
63. Candy Corn Relay 82
64. Pass It Fast Relay 83
65. Ghostly Platter Relay................................. 84
66. Magical Stick Relay 85
67. Halloween Balloon Pop 86
68. Back To Back Relay................................... 87
69. Mysterious Relay.. 88

Spooktacular Active Games

70. Mummy Wrap Game.................................... 90
71. Balloon Stuff Game..................................... 91
72. Suspended Apple Race 92
73. Halloween Scavenger Hunt 94
74. Flying Ghost Game 95
75. Devilish Video Scavenger Hunt 96
76. Pass The Spider Race 98

Spooktacular Quiet Games

77. Stick The Nose On The Pumpkin........................ 100
78. Bobbing For Apples 101
79. Spooky Feel It Game.................................. 102
80. Halloween Bingo... 104
81. Guessing Game... 105
82. Halloween Candy Drop 106
83. Eyeball Toss 107
84. Skeleton Hang Man 108
85. Halloween Word Hunt................................. 109
86. Spooky Word Scramble.............................. 110
87. Creepy Word Search 112

SPOOKTACULAR PARTY FAVORS AND CRAFTS

88. Bouncing Eye Balls 116
89. Ghost Suckers 117
90. Paper Sack Pumpkins 118
91. Fuzzy Spiders 119
92. Ghostly Stick-Ons 120
93. Bare Bones Skeletons 122
94. Ghostly Wind Sock 124
95. Slime 126
96. Halloween Sugar Art 128
97. Play Dough Pumpkins 129
98. Nut Cup Spiders 130
99. Handy Treats 131
100. Black Cat Party Favors 132
101. Freaky Beady Spider 134

LIST OF FIGURES

Figure 1   Sample epitaphs 11
Figure 2   Monster footprint sample 14
Figure 3   Examples of Sinister Yard Signs 15
Figure 4   Sample spider eye 18
Figure 5   Examples of messages for Creepy Signs 20
Figure 6   Flying Bats pattern 23
Figure 7   Stencil pattern for Spider Web Brownies 60
Figure 8   How to suspend an apple by a string 93
Figure 9   Spider leg example 119
Figure 10 Ghost pattern 121
Figure 11 How to assemble the skeleton 123
Figure 12 Spider leg example 130
Figure 13 Black cat patterns 133
Figure 14 How to string the beads together 135
Figure 15 Bead pattern 135
Figure 16 How to bend the spider's legs 135

INTRODUCTION

Hosting a Halloween party at your home is the perfect way to have a ghoulishly delightful get-together with family, friends and neighbors. It takes a lot of planning and advance preparation to pull off a truly memorable evening, so get the entire family involved and try to keep it simple.

101 Spooktacular Party Ideas includes ideas that will help you haunt your house with boo-tiful decorations, serve sinisterly delectable treats, play bone chilling games and make fiendishly fun crafts. Use them as offered — or adapt them for your own special needs.

Each party idea is written in an easy-to-read format that includes the following:

Idea Introduction:
Suggests a way to use the idea at your party.

List Of Materials:
A detailed list of all materials needed to complete the project or activity is included with each idea. Most of the materials are easy to find either at home or at a local grocery, department or craft store.

How -To Instructions:
Simple step-by-step directions are provided to help guide you through the entire activity. When helpful, I have included advance preparation steps. This allows you to be prepared, which is an important step to help make your party a success.

Read through the following ideas and have a great time planning your Halloween party. Remember to be creative and let your imagination run wild.

MOST OF ALL, MAKE IT FUN!

HELPFUL SUGGESTIONS

Planning The Party:

- Plan a party that will not only be fun for your guests, but fun for you as well. If you try to take on more than you can handle, you will feel stressed and you probably won't have a good time. Remember, your party doesn't have to be a fancy affair. There are plenty of ideas in this book, but don't feel guilty if you decide to host a simple party using only a few of the ideas. Plan the type of party that feels good to you and your guests will have a wonderful time!

- Be sure to give yourself plenty of time to plan your party. Four weeks is usually enough time to get your house decorated, invitations sent and supplies purchased.

- Pick and choose ideas that are appropriate for the ages of your guests. Adults and older children will usually find a haunted house to be thrilling and fun, while younger children can become very disturbed and frightened. If you will be hosting a mix of ages, set up the scariest decorations and activities out of sight of the main party. The Disembodied Heads (Idea # 15), for example, can be set up in a remote closet so that younger kids will avoid seeing them.

- When planning a party, timing is critical. Parties are a time of excitement and a child's attention span tends to be short. If you are planning a children's party, you might include a few games, some treats and a fun craft that can be taken home as a party favor.

Planning The Games:

- Plan more games than you think you will need in case some of them turn out to be too difficult or do not appeal to your guests. If your guests are having fun with a game, let them continue to play. If they appear to be bored, move on to the next game.

- Try to alternate quiet and active games. By doing this, you maintain a desirable energy level among your guests and prevent them from getting overly excited or bored.

- Make sure you have plenty of room to play the games that you have chosen.

- Since people tend to be clumsy in their costumes, make sure that anything fragile or sharp is well out of the way. Do this throughout your house, not just in the game area.

Game Prizes:

- You will need to decide whether or not to offer prizes. If you do award prizes, try to make sure that everyone receives one. Simple, inexpensive prizes such as spider rings, Halloween pencils, ghost erasers and Halloween stickers work well for children. Consider nonmaterial prizes, such as going first in the next game or receiving a round of applause from the group. Older children enjoy dividing into teams and keeping track of the points earned. When the games are complete, each member of each team should receive a prize.

- Adult prizes might include Halloween items such as candles, skulls, pumpkins, fuzzy bats, etc. If you are having an adults only party, consider asking each guest to bring a wrapped Halloween item that will be used for game or door prizes. Wrapped 'white elephant' gifts are also a lot of fun.

Planning The Treats:

- When trying to figure out how much food to prepare for your party, it's a good idea to plan on the high side. If you have food left over, send it home with your guests or save it for your family—you won't have to cook again for a few days!

- Consider the ages of your guests when deciding on the amount of food you will need. Young children are often too excited to bother with food at parties. Make portions small and serve seconds if needed.

- To help prevent spills, make sure all of the children are seated before their drinks are poured. It is also a good idea to fill their cups half full.

- Do not serve beverages that stain, such as grape juice.

Safety Reminders:

- If children are going to be at the party, I suggest using flashlights or light sticks rather than candles. Also, keep dry ice out of the reach of the children. They will play in it, which can be dangerous.

- Carefully monitor all activities involving children and scissors. I strongly suggest using safety scissors for all of the craft projects.

- Hot glue guns are recommended for a number of the craft projects. It is very important that ADULTS ONLY use the hot glue guns. Always exercise extreme caution when using a glue gun.

- When using balloons, make sure that children play with only the inflated and intact balloons. Immediately dispose of all balloons that break. Swallowed or inhaled balloons or balloon pieces present a serious suffocation threat.

SPOOKTACULAR OUTDOOR DECORATIONS

Whether you have a large yard and porch, or simply a small entryway, there are many decorations that can be used outside to greet your party guests. The ideas in this chapter will help you haunt your yard and set the spooky mood for your party and trick-or-treaters.

Begin by lining your driveway or sidewalk with *Sinister Yard Signs* and *Halloween Luminaries*. If you have a yard, why not turn part of it into a haunted graveyard. Build a small *Picket Fence*, make some creative *Tombstones* and don't forget the eerie *Fresh Gravesites*. Just for fun, draw some *Monster Footprints* on your sidewalk to lead the way to your front door. Of course, don't forget to hang some *Flying Ghosts* in your trees.

HAPPY HAUNTING!

Haunted Graveyard No haunted

house would be complete without it's very own haunted graveyard. Start with a picket fence, add tombstones, a partially buried body, spider webs and voila! You'll have an instant graveyard.

Idea # 1
Picket Fence

Idea # 2
Tombstones

Idea # 3
Fresh
Gravesite

IDEA #1

Picket Fence

How To Make It:

1. Paint the stakes and trim boards.
2. Lay out your graveyard using the string.
3. Cut the trim boards the correct lengths to go around your graveyard.
4. Measuring down approximately 5" from the top of each stake, draw a line with the pencil.
5. Using the line on each stake as a guide, nail the trim boards to each stake. Space them about every 12 inches.
6. Pound the stakes into the ground to finish your graveyard fence.

Supply List

18" or 24" **Wood Stakes**
1" **Trim Boards**
¾" **Nails**
White Exterior House Paint

___

String, Measuring Tape, Hammer, Paint Brush, Saw, Pencil

IDE A #2

Tombstones

How To Make Them:

1. Cut the Styrofoam sheets into various size rectangles. Mine ranged in size from 13"x 13" to 13"x 21".
2. With a knife, cut the top corners of each stone so they are rounded. Cut one side first, then use that piece as a pattern for the second side.
3. Paint all sides of your tombstone gray.
4. When dry, write an epitaph on each tombstone with the black marker. Use some of the epitaphs in Figure 1, or create your own messages.
5. Glue the tombstones to the stakes using a hot glue gun. Make sure the bottom of each tombstone is at least 6" above the bottom point of each stake.
6. Carefully pound the stakes into the ground until the bottom of each tombstone is just above the ground.

Supply List

3/4" sheet of **Styrofoam**
King size **Black Permanent Marker**
Gray Acrylic Paint
Wood Stakes
Hot Glue Gun
———
Serrated Knife, Paint Brush, Hammer

RIP

Rick R. Mortis

Here Lies Bob Yeast He's Sure To Rise Again

RIP

Barry D' Alive

Here Lies I.B. Happy She Died Laughing

RIP

Here Lies Harry Monster

Figure 1: Sample epitaphs.

IDEA #3

Fresh Gravesites *These gravesites will make it look like some 'unexpected guests' may be joining you.*

How To Make Them:

1. Cut the black plastic bag to the approximate size of the gravesite. It will go under the soil or pine bark so cleanup is easy.
2. Shovel the soil or pine bark on top of the black plastic bag. Mound it up so it looks like a freshly dug grave.
3. Place the gloves on top of the gravesite where a person's hands would be.
4. Place the shoes at the bottom of the gravesite. To help them stick up, place soil or pine bark inside each shoe. Your gravesite should look as if someone was recently partially buried there.
5. In the dirt or pine bark, hide a flashlight so that it is positioned to shine directly on your grave's tombstone at night.

Supply List

Fresh **Soil** or **Pine Bark**
Large **Black Plastic Bag**
Pair of **Old Gloves**
Pair of **Old Shoes**
Flashlight
————
Shovel, Scissors

IDEA #4

Halloween Luminaries *Cast a ghostly glow along your front walkway with these easy luminaries. What a great way to recycle those McDonald® Halloween Happy Meal buckets.*

How To Make Them:

1. Fill each bucket about 1/3 full with sand.
2. Place the votive candle in the middle of the sand.
3. Line your sidewalk with the buckets.
4. Carefully light each candle.

Supply List

Small **Halloween** or **Pumpkin Buckets**
Votive Candles
Sand

IDEA #5

Headless Ghoul *Place this scary creature on the front porch to greet your party guests and trick-or-treaters.*

Supply List

1 scary **Monster Mask**
1 set of **Old Clothes**: shirt, pants or
 overalls
1 pair of **Old Boots**
1 pair of **Old Gloves**
1 **Black Trash Bag**

Newspapers, Safety Pins, Scissors,
Tape, Old Chair

How To Make It:

1. Place an old chair in a corner on your front porch.
2. Stuff the monster mask with newspaper.
3. Button up the front of the shirt and stuff with newspapers. Don't overstuff! You want the arms to be able to bend and hold the monster mask on the ghoul's lap.
4. Cover the newspaper that is visible in the neck area with part of a black plastic bag and tuck the bag under the shirt.
5. Stuff the pants with newspaper until they are plump.
6. Tuck the shirt into the pants and use safety pins as needed to keep the shirt and pants together.
7. Fill each glove with newspaper and insert into the shirt cuffs. Use safety pins to keep in place if necessary.
8. Position your ghoul's body so it is sitting in the chair. If necessary, use tape to ensure that it stays in the chair.
9. Put the boots on the ground in front of the chair and pull the bottom of each pant leg down over each boot.
10. Place the monster mask in your ghoul's lap and position the hands so it appears as if they are holding the head.

IDEA #6

Monster Footprints Guide

trick-or-treaters to your door with these spooky footprints.

How To Make Them:

1. Draw a monster's footprint on a piece of cardboard. Use the example in Figure 2, or create your own.
2. Cut the footprint out of the middle of the piece of cardboard. It should look like a stencil.
3. With the chalk, trace the footprint onto your sidewalk and color in completely.
4. Turn the stencil over to make the next footprint.
5. Continue tracing and coloring footprints all the way to your front door.

> ### Supply List
>
> Glow in the Dark **Chalk**
> **Cardboard**
> _____
> **Pencil, Scissors**

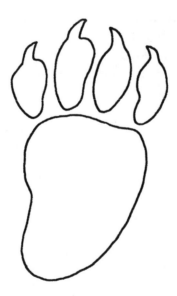

Figure 2: Monster footprint sample.

IDEA #7

Sinister Yard Signs *Guide your Halloween guests to your haunted house with these creepy signs.*

How To Make Them:

1. Decide what size and shapes you want your signs to be. Cut the cardboard to the appropriate sizes and shapes. Most of my signs were 8" x 16".
2. With a pencil, write a 'warning' on each sign. You can use the examples in Figure 3, or create your own.
3. Paint each of the words on your sign with very wide letters. To give them a ghoulish look, let the bottom of each letter 'melt' down a little bit.
4. Place the reflective tape on your sign. It can be used as a border or to make an arrow to point your visitors in the right direction.
5. Hot glue your sign to a wood stake.
6. Hammer your signs into the ground.

Supply List

Florescent or Glow in
the Dark **Paints**
Cardboard
18" Wood Stakes
Hot Glue Gun
Black Reflective Tape
_____

**Pencil, Paint Brush,
Scissors, Hammer**

Figure 3: Examples of Sinister Yard Signs.

IDEA #8

Flying Ghosts Hang a small group of these ghosts from a tree to welcome your Halloween guests.

Supply List

White Plastic **Trash Bags**
6" or 9" **White Balloons**
Newspapers
White String
Clear Tape
Black Permanent Marker

Scissors, Large Needle

How To Make Them:

1. For the head of your ghost, blow up a white balloon and knot the end.
2. Place the balloon 'head' inside the white plastic trash bag.
3. Gather the plastic trash bag around the bottom of the 'head' and tie off at the neck with a piece of string.
4. Use tape to hold the corners down on top of the 'head'.
5. With a permanent black marker, draw a face on your ghost.
6. With a large needle, thread a long piece of string through the top of the ghost's head and tie together. Be careful not to pop the balloon. You might want to reinforce the area around the string with tape if it is going to be windy outside.
7. Shred the bottom of the trash bag for a spooky effect.
8. Suspend from a low branch in a large tree.

Suggestions:

- These ghosts also look great hanging inside your haunted house.
- Fill the balloons with helium and let them 'hang around' the inside of your house, or tie them to chairs and tables.
- You could also put a few helium filled ghosts in a box. When guests open the box, the ghosts will float up and scare them!

IDEA #9

Humongous Spiders It is fun to
watch the faces of people passing by when they stop to look at this huge spider sitting on your porch or lawn.

Supply List

5— Large **Black Plastic Trash Bags** with twist ties
1— 8½"x 11" sheet of **Bright Yellow Paper**
Lots of **Newspapers**
Black Electrical Tape

Scissors, Pencil, Double Sided Carpet Tape

How To Make Them:

1. To make the body, stuff one trash bag with newspapers until it is full and round. Twist the bottom to close and secure with tape or a twist tie.
2. To make a leg, cut a trash bag down both long sides. Open the bag so it lies flat and forms a large rectangle.
3. Tape the two long ends together.
4. Twist the middle of the bag a few times to form a knee joint.
5. Crumble the newspapers and stuff them inside the open ends until full.
6. Twist both ends and secure with tape or a twist tie.
7. Repeat steps 2-6 with the remaining three trash bags.
8. On the yellow piece of paper draw the spider's eyes. You may copy the sample in Figure 4 or create your own.
9. Cut out the eyes.
10. Using the carpet tape, tape the eyes onto the round trash bag.
11. Take your spider parts outside to be assembled. Use the black tape to secure the four jointed legs to the spider's body.

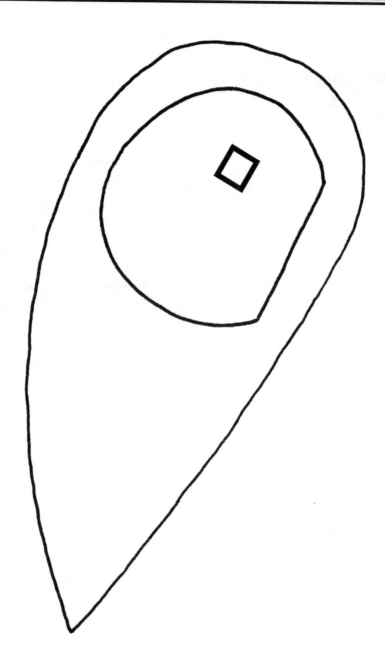

Figure 4: Sample spider eye.

SPOOKTACULAR INDOOR DECORATIONS

This section contains some great ideas for decorations that will help you haunt your house. Some of them are easy to do, while others are fairly complex. Choose the ideas that are appropriate for the ages of your guests. If you will be hosting a mix of ages, set up the scariest decorations out of sight of the main party area to avoid frightening the young children. The *Open If You Dare Box* (Idea #14) or *Disembodied Heads* (Idea #15), for example, can be set up in a remote closet or bathroom so that younger children can avoid seeing them.

The following ideas serve as suggestions that may inspire your own ideas. Don't overdo the decorations. You can have a memorable Halloween party without having every corner of your house decorated. Try to keep it simple, safe and fun.

IDEA #10

Creepy Signs *Signs hung on doors around your house will add to your haunted décor and will make exploring your house even more fun for party goers.*

How To Make Them:

Supply List

Florescent or Glow in the Dark **Paints**
Cardboard
Reusable Adhesive
———
Pencil, Paint Brush, Scissors

1. Decide what size and shapes you want your signs to be. Cut the cardboard to the appropriate sizes and shapes. Most of my signs were 6"x 11".
2. With a pencil, write a 'warning' on each sign. You can use some of the examples in Figure 5, or create your own.
3. Paint each of the words onto your sign with very wide letters. To give them a ghoulish look, let the bottom of each letter 'melt' down a little bit.
4. Place a dime size piece of reusable adhesive to the back of each corner of your sign and stick to a door or wall.

Warning: Enter At Your Own Risk!	Do Not Enter: Experiments In Progress!
Danger!	**Go Away!**
KEEP OUT!	OPEN IF YOU DARE!

Figure 5: Examples of messages for Creepy Signs.

IDEA #11

Friendly Ghosts *For a not so*
scary decoration, make this pair of ghosts and set them in front of your fireplace. Don't build a fire!

Supply List

2 bags of **Cheese Cloth**
2 **White Trash Bags**
2 large **White Balloons**
1 large **Hair Bow**
Newspapers
Wide **Black Electrical Tape**

───────

Scissors, Iron , Ironing Board

How To Make Them:

1. Unfold the cheese cloth and with an iron on low heat, iron out wrinkles.
2. Blow up the balloons and knot the ends.
3. Place one balloon in each white trash bag.
4. Fill the rest of the trash bag with crinkled newspapers. Form the trash bag to look like the outline of a ghost's body. The balloon will be on top and form the head, while the newspaper will support the head and form the body.
5. Drape a piece of cheese cloth over the ghost. You should have enough cheese cloth to double the layers on each ghost.
6. Cut four round eyes out of the black electrical tape.
7. Place two of the eyes on each ghost.
8. Make a girl ghost by taping a large hair bow to the top of one of the ghost's head.

Suggestion:

- Purchase cotton spider webs from your local store and stretch them all around your ghosts. The more you stretch the webbing, the more authentic the cobweb will look.

IDEA #12

Flying Bats *Dangle these bats from your ceilings and doorways for a delightfully eerie effect.*

Supply List

For each bat you will need:
- 1/2 sheet **Brown Construction Paper**
- **Yellow** and **Brown Crayons**
- **Black Marker**
- 36" piece of **Black String**

Scissors, Pencil, Tracing Paper, Cardboard, Glue

How To Make It:

1. With the tracing paper, copy the bat pattern in Figure 6 and cut out.
2. Copy this pattern onto the piece of cardboard and cut out.
3. Fold the construction paper in half length wise.
4. Using the cardboard pattern, trace the half bat onto the piece of construction paper. Be sure to note where the dashed fold lines are located.
5. Cut out the bat.
6. Cut out the bat's feet by following the lines that are shown in Figure 6.
7. Use the black marker and brown crayon to make a fancy bat. Color the bat as shown in the above picture. Use the yellow crayon to color in the eyes.
8. Fold along the dashed lines. The body will fold up and the wings will fold down.
9. Poke a small hole where the dot is on the pattern.
10. Cut a 36" piece of black string. Thread the string through the small hole and tie a large knot on the back side of the bat.
11. Repeat on the other side of the bat.
12. Hang in a doorway or from the ceiling.

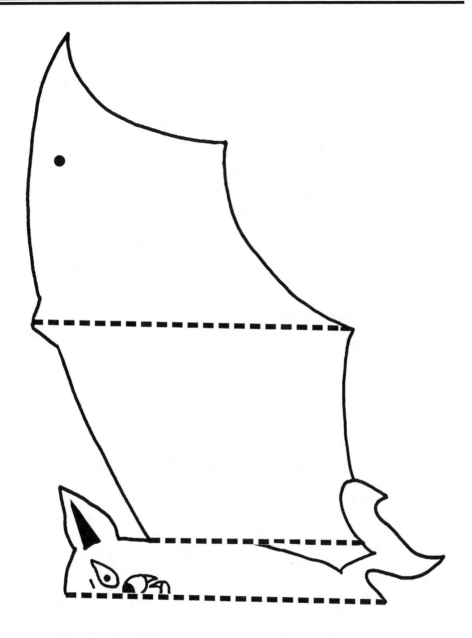

Figure 6: Flying Bats pattern.

IDEA #13

Streamers *This decoration makes a fun separator between rooms or at the bottom of stairways.*

Supply List

Black Streamers
Orange Streamers
Black String

Scissors, Clear Tape

How To Make Them:

1. With a long piece of streamer, measure from the top of the doorway to the floor and cut with the scissors.
2. Use this piece of streamer as a guide and cut pieces of black and orange streamers all the same length. Half of the streamers will be orange and half will be black.
3. With the string, measure across the top of the doorway. Add two inches to that length and cut.
4. Beginning about one inch from the end of the string, fold one inch of one end of a streamer over the string and staple together.
5. Repeat step 4, alternating black and orange streamers, until the string is full. Push the streamers together as you work.
6. Use the tape to hang the string across the doorway.

Variations:

- Cut the streamers to varying lengths for a less uniform look.
- Use only one color of streamer.
- Place the streamers along windows to cut down on the amount of light in the room.

IDEA #14

Open If You Dare Box *Your*
guests will not be able to resist the temptation to look
inside this haunting box.

Supply List

1 gross looking **Skeleton Mask**
1 pair of **Skeleton Gloves**
1 large **Box**
1 small **Box**
1 can of **Black Spray Paint**
1 **Black Trash Bag**
Newspapers
1 *"Open If You Dare"* **Sign**

———

Tape, Stapler

How To Make It:

1. Spray paint the large box black. Let dry. If there is a lot of printing on the box you might have to apply a second coat of paint.
2. Open the top of the large box and place the small box inside. The top of the small box needs to sit about 6 inches below the top of the large box. If necessary, use scrunched up newspapers to raise the small box.
3. Fill in the space around the small box with scrunched up newspapers.
4. Drape the black trash bag over the top of the small box and newspapers.
5. Stuff newspaper into the skeleton mask to make it look like a head.
6. Place the skeleton mask on top of the small box. When you open the top of the large box, the gross skeleton head should be looking up at you.
7. Position the pair of skeleton hands on the large box so that they look like they are coming out of the box. Staple in place.
8. Tape the "Open If You Dare" sign (see Idea # 10) above the box.

IDEA #15

Disembodied Heads *Find the*
grossest masks possible, hang them in a closet and watch
your guests get scared out of their pants.

Supply List

2 or more scary **Masks**
8 feet of **Rope**
1 **White Sheet**
Newspapers
1 *"Do Not Enter!"* **Sign**
___

Scissors, Tape, Push Pins

How To Make Them:

1. Crumble newspapers and stuff into the masks until they are full.
2. Cut the rope in half.
3. Tape a piece of rope securely to the top of each mask.
4. In the closet where your heads will hang, secure the ropes to the door frame with push pins. Adjust the length of the ropes so the heads will hang one above the other. Cut off leftover rope.
5. With the push pins, tack the sheet to the inside of the door frame.
6. Tape the back of the heads to the sheet to keep them from turning around.
7. Tape a "Do Not Enter!" sign (see Idea # 10) on the front of the closet door.

Suggestions:

- The scarier the masks the better.
- Do not use open backed masks because they are difficult to stuff.

IDEA #16

 Haunted Tunnel *To get your party off to a thrilling start, have your guests enter your house through the garage where you have setup this haunted tunnel. Eeeek!*

Supply List

Large refrigerator or other   **Duct Tape**
    appliance **Boxes**   **Staple Gun**
Black Streamers   **Clear Tape**
Dry Beans   **Sheet Rock Knife**
Plastic Rats and **Spiders**   **Tacks**
Black Paint (Optional)   **Sheet**

How To Make It:

1. If you have a lot of time, it is fun to paint the inside top and sides of the boxes with black paint. This is a great effect. If the maze is in a dark area, it really isn't necessary.

2. With the duct tape and staple gun, fasten your boxes together, end to end, and run the tunnel through the garage. Make sure the first box is just inside a door. If you have enough boxes, you can form a maze that includes dead ends to make it more confusing.

3. Between two boxes, hang some black streamers from the top of the boxes. They should hang down just enough to brush against your guest's faces. Tape the two boxes together.

4. Pour some dry beans on the floor of a box so your guests have to crawl through them. It will feel gross, but won't make a big mess.

5. Place the plastic spiders and rats throughout the tunnel.

6. For some really scary thrills, cut some holes in the tunnel wall using the sheet rock knife. A glove covered hand can thrust through the holes to grab at your guests as they pass by.

7. At the door leading into your tunnel, tack or tape a sheet from the top of the doorway and drape it over the first box.

8. On the sheet, hang a sign that says "Enter If You Dare!" (see Idea # 10). For young children and those who do not 'Dare' to enter, provide an alternate way to get to your party.

IDEA #17

Candy Corn Candles *For a sweeter alternative to the jack-o-lantern candles, set out some of these candy corn votives.*

Supply List

1 large **Bowl**
1 large bag of **Candy Corn**
1 small glass **Votive**
1 **Tea Light**

How To Make It:

1. Fill the bowl almost to the top with candy corn.
2. Place the small glass votive inside the bowl so that the top of the votive is even with the top of the bowl.
3. Fill in the space around the votive with candy.
4. Place the tea light inside the votive.

Suggestions:

- Do not reach in for any of the candy until you blow out the candle.
- If children are attending your party, place this and all candles out of their reach.
- Use a large jar instead of a bowl.

Did You Know?

The word Halloween means *hallowed* or *holy evening* because it takes place the day before All Saints' Day.

Spooktacular Lighting Cast
a ghostly glow throughout your haunted house with these lighting ideas.

Supply List

Any or all of the following:
- **Black Light Bulbs**
- **Orange** and **Yellow Colored Light Bulbs**
- **Strings of Black** or **Orange Lights**
- **Candles**—black, orange, skull, pumpkin, etc.
- **Flashlights**

- Turn the lights down low. The darker the better — as long as you don't create an unsafe environment.

- Replace regular light bulbs with orange or yellow colored light bulbs.

- What would a Halloween party be without black lights? They create an awesome effect when glow-in-the-dark spider webs, skeletons and signs are decorating the same room. The surprising thing is that they do not give out very much light. Try to use them in a small room — a bathroom or narrow hallway works great. Be careful when working with black light bulbs, they get **very** hot.

- Hang strings of purple or orange lights (they are just like Christmas lights) around the windows and stairways of your haunted house. Check the labels to make sure they are suitable for indoor use.

- Give children flashlights. Turn out all the lights and let them find their way around your haunted house using only their flashlights.

- Place orange and black candles throughout your house. Place them in candelabras or in Halloween themed candle holders. For a really gross effect, check your local novelty store for some of the new candles that look like skulls. When they melt, red candle wax runs out of their eyes and mouth. Yuck!

  Always use extreme caution when using candles. Follow the directions on the candles and keep them out of the reach of all children. If children are attending your party do **NOT** light the candles, simply use them as decorations.

- For an eerie glow, cover lampshades with green or orange crepe paper. You can also cover recessed lights with orange crepe paper. Make sure the crepe paper you are using is flame retardant because the lights can get very hot!

- For a safe alternative to candles, use flashlights and light sticks.

- Place yellow or green cellophane or plastic wrap over the bulb end of a flashlight for an eerie effect. Use rubber bands to hold the plastic wrap in place. These look great shining in the corners of a dark room.

Did You Know?

Dracula is the name of a book written by Bram Stoker in 1897. It is one of the most famous horror stories of all time. The book's main character is Count Dracula. He is a nobleman who is really a *vampire*.

IDEA #19

Small Touches *Your decorations do not have to be elaborate or expensive. Try these easy decorating ideas.*

Supply List

Any or all of the following:
Plastic Rats, Spiders, Snakes
Large Paper or **Plastic Skeletons**
Balloons
Dead Flowers
Fake Spider Confetti
Black Spider Rings
Cotton Spider Webs
White Sheets

- You can really spook your guests with life-like plastic rats, spiders and snakes. Put them in odd places where they will least expect them. You might put them on top of the towels in the bathroom, in a soap dish, behind the bathroom door, or hang them from a light or light switch. Be creatively creepy.

- Hang a life-size skeleton in a closet. To really make it stand out, hang a black plastic bag behind it.

- Balloons are a fun touch to any Halloween Party. Children enjoy drawing pumpkin faces on orange balloons with permanent black markers. You can fill the bathtub with orange and black balloons, or just hang them all around your house.

- A few days before your party, ask a local florist to save any dead flowers that would usually be thrown away. On the day of the party, put them in vases and place them around the house.

- To create a creepy aura on your food table, sprinkle it with spider confetti. You can also put some in the party invitations that you send.

- Purchase orange plastic silverware for your party and use a black plastic spider ring to keep the place settings together.

- At a local store, purchase some bags of cotton spider webs. This is a very inexpensive decoration that can be used throughout your house. The secret is to separate the webbing into long strands and to stretch them as far as possible. For a real haunted house look, fasten the webs to the corners of shelving, across the facing of cabinets, into the cracks of your fireplace brick and around lamps or most any object. Use it all over and let your children help.

- What would a haunted house be without a bunch of old furniture. Make your nice furniture look creepy by covering it with old white sheets.

- Place Boiling Caldrons (Idea #53) around your haunted house. While this makes a terrific eerie effect, it is fairly labor intensive to keep it boiling. It should **only** be used at an **adults only** party because of the dangers associated with dry ice.

Helpful Suggestion:

Have a camera and plenty of film available to take pictures of your costumed guests as they arrive. For a fun take-home party favor, take instant photo's of your guests.

QUICK & EASY SPOOKTACULAR TREATS

Cool Eyeballs, *Dirt Cups*, *Graveyard Ghosts*, *Goblins Nutty Mix* and *Witches Hats* — they're all scrumptious treats. These bone-chilling goodies are not tricky to make and they are sure to be a big hit at your Halloween bash. These treats are especially designed so that your young guests can 'create' their own special Halloween treat.

Enjoy!

IDEA #20

Cool Eyeballs *If there are children coming to your Halloween party, make sure this is one of the treats served. Make them ahead of time, or let each child make their own.*

Recipe Will Make: 10 Cool Eyeballs.

Supply List

1 tub (8 oz.) of frozen **Whipped Topping**
10 pieces of **Life Saver® Candies**
1 tube of **Red Gel Frosting**

Ice Cream Scoop, Aluminum Foil, Cookie Sheet

How To Make Them:

1. Line a cookie sheet (make sure it will fit in your freezer) with aluminum foil.
2. With an ice cream scoop, place 10 large scoops of frozen whipped topping on the aluminum foil. These are going to be the 'eyeballs', so make them as round as possible.
3. Place the 'eyeballs' in the freezer for 30 minutes or until firm.
4. Just before serving, remove from the freezer.
5. Transfer the 'eyeballs' to a serving platter.
6. Place a Life Saver® in the middle of each 'eyeball' for the pupil.
7. With the red gel frosting, draw blood veins radiating out from the candy pupils.

Suggestions:

- This is an easy treat for children to make. Instead of placing the 'eyeballs' in the freezer, serve them up on plastic plates and let the children decorate their own 'eyeball'.
- Do not let these sit out for more than 15 minutes; they will melt.
- Vanilla ice cream can be substituted for the whipped topping.

Dirt Cups *Let the children make these delightfully gross treats themselves.*

Supply List
Oreo® Cookies
Chocolate Pudding
Gummy Worms
Clear **Plastic Cups**

Plastic Spoons, Wax Paper,
Mixing Bowls, Rolling Pin,
Airtight Container, Large
Spoon

Advance Preparations:
▶ Crush the cookies using the wax paper and rolling pin. When you are finished, it should resemble lumpy black dirt.
▶ Store in an airtight container.
▶ Prepare the chocolate pudding according to the directions on the package. Cover and refrigerate.
▶ If you have time, make a sample by following the steps below. The children will get excited when they see what they are going to make.

How To Make It:
1. You will be making this treat by alternating layers of cookie crumbs and pudding. Start by putting a spoonful of crushed cookies in the bottom of a plastic cup.
2. Next, add a few spoonfuls of chocolate pudding.
3. Now add a worm or two.
4. Continue with another layer of cookies and then pudding.
5. Top it off with a cookie layer and some worms.
6. With a spoon, 'Dig In'!

IDEA #22

Bugs On A Log *These appetizers might sound unusual, but your guests will really eat-em-up.*

Recipe Will Make: A lot of logs and even more bugs.

Supply List

Celery
Peanut Butter
Raisins
Mini Chocolate Chips

Spoon, Knife, Paper Towels

How To Make It:

1. Wash the celery and pat dry with paper towels.
2. Cut celery into pieces (about 4 inches long).
3. With a knife, spread the peanut butter on the celery.
4. On half of the celery sticks, press raisins randomly into the peanut butter. They should look like little bugs on a log.
5. On the remaining celery sticks, press mini chocolate chips randomly into the peanut butter.
6. They are now ready to serve.

Variations:

- Instead of peanut butter, spread pimiento cheese spread on the celery. For the bugs, press chopped pimientos and green or black olives.
- You could also use jalapeno cheese spread on the celery. For the bugs use either chopped jalapenos or black olives.

IDEA #23

Caramel Apples *This classic Halloween treat is especially fun when children get to decorate them with candy corn.*

Supply List

Apples	Caramels
Candy Corn	Craft Sticks
Shortening	

Crock Pot, Large Spoon, Knife, Small Plastic Plates, Sandwich Bags

Advance Preparations:

▶ Wash apples.

▶ Unwrap caramels and put in the crock pot. Check the recipe on the bag to see if water needs to be added to the caramels.

▶ Heat the caramel and have it melted in time for the party.

How To Make It:

1. Push a craft stick into the top of each apple.
2. Spread a little shortening on each small plastic plate. This will help to keep the apples from sticking to the plate.
3. **Carefully** dip apples into the melted caramel. It is **HOT**! While holding the stick, twirl the apple until it is covered with caramel.
4. Place the apples on the small plastic plates.
5. Decorate with candy corn.
6. After cooling for a few minutes, the children can either eat them or take them home in a plastic bag. Have a knife handy in case the children want their apples cut up for easy eating.

IDEA #24

Spider Treats *Young ghosts and goblins will have as much fun assembling these spider treats as they will eating them.*

Recipe Will Make: 10 Spiders Treats.

Supply List
10 **Marshmallow Pies**
30 pieces of **Black Licorice**
20 miniature **Marshmallows**
20 **Chocolate Chips**
Vanilla or **Chocolate Frosting**

Paper Plates, Knife

Advance Preparations:

► Cut each piece of licorice in half.
► Using the directions below, make a sample spider treat so the children can see what they will be making.
► Before the party begins, spread out the paper plates and place on each plate: 1 marshmallow pie, 6 pieces of licorice, 2 marshmallows and 2 chocolate chips. In addition, place a small amount of frosting on each plate.

How To Make It:

1. Give each child a paper plate.
2. Show the children the sample spider treat.
3. Tell the children that the marshmallow pie will be the body, the black licorice will be the legs, the marshmallows will be the eyes and the chocolate chips will be the eyeballs. They will use the frosting as glue to make the eyes and eyeballs stick to their spider.
4. Have the children assemble their 'spiders'.
5. Dig in!

Suggestion:

• Since many children do not like the taste of black licorice, substitute one of the new fruit flavored licorice's for the spider's legs.

IDEA #25

Witches Hats *These sweet treats are a super addition to any Halloween gathering!*

Recipe Will Make: 24 Witches Hats.

Supply List

24 **Chocolate Wafer Cookies**
24 **Hershey Kisses**®
1 tube of **Orange Decorating Icing**

Small Round Frosting Tip

How To Make Them:
1. Unwrap the Hershey Kisses®.
2. With the orange frosting, squeeze a dime size portion in the center of each cookie.
3. Place a Hershey Kiss® on the icing.
4. Complete the hats by piping some frosting around the base of each Kiss and drawing a small square buckle.

IDEA #26

Goblins Nutty Mix *Your guests will enjoy this tongue-tingling mixture of salty nuts and sweet candy. Many people think it tastes like a Butterfinger*® *candy bar.*

Supply List

1 package of **Spanish Peanuts** (with skins)
1 package of **Candy Corn**

Air Tight Container

How To Make It:
1. Simply mix the peanuts and candy corn together in the container.

IDEA #27

Graveyard Ghosts *Your young goblin guests will have a haunting good time making their own delicious graveyard treats.*

Supply List

Brownies
Small rectangular **Cookies**
Whipped Topping
Miniature **Chocolate Chips**
Candy Corn and **Pumpkins**
Red Jel Frosting

Paper Plates, Spoons, Napkins

Advance Preparations:
On the day of the party:
▶ Decorate the rectangular cookies (tombstones) by writing "BOO" or "RIP" on them with the red jel frosting.
▶ Set up an area where the children will make their grave-yard ghosts. Place all of the food on the table buffet style: brownies and tombstone cookies first, followed by the whipped topping, chocolate chips, candy corn and candy pumpkins.

How To Make It:
1. Give each child a paper plate and napkin.
2. If you have a large number of children, divide them into groups of five.
3. Have one group at a time go to the table to assemble their treat.
4. The following steps explain how to create the graveyard ghosts:
    A. Place a brownie on the paper plate.
    B. Stick one or two 'tombstone' cookies in the brownie.
    C. Stack a few spoonfuls of whipped topping in the shape of a ghost on top of the brownie. Add two miniature choco-late chips for the eyes.
    D. Complete the graveyard scene with candy corn and candy pumpkins.

Spooktacular Fruit Pizza

These individual treats can be prepared with whatever toppings each child prefers.

Supply List

Large **Sugar Cookies** (5"- 6")
Whipped Topping
Fruit—bananas, grapes, peaches, strawberries, kiwi, pineapple
Orange **Food Coloring**

Paper Plates, Large Spoons, Large Bowls, Gallon Size Zip-Top Plastic Bags

Advance Preparations:

▶ Bake or purchase <u>large</u> (5"- 6") cookies.

On the day of the party:

▶ Wash and slice the fresh fruit. Store in zip-top bags. Wait to slice the bananas until the children are ready to eat.
▶ Drain and slice the canned fruit. Store in zip-top bags.
▶ Thaw whipped topping. Add food coloring until bright orange. Refrigerate.

At the party:

▶ Pour each bag of fruit into a bowl.
▶ Place all of the food and supplies on a table buffet style: Paper plates and cookies first, followed by the whipped topping and fruit.

How To Make It:

1. If you have a large number of children, divide them into groups of five.
2. Send one group at a time to the table to assemble their fruit pizza. Start by placing one large spoonful of whipped topping on the cookie, followed by the fruit of their choice.

IDEA #29

 Monster Crunch This Halloween

treat starts out as a gooey mess and ends up as a snack that is hard to resist. Children enjoy 'shaking' it themselves!

Recipe Will Make: A bunch of Monster Crunch.

Supply List
1 box of **Crispix®** or **Chex®** Cereal
1 <u>stick</u> of **Margarine**
1 cup of **Peanut Butter**
12 oz bag **Chocolate Chips**
1 bag **Powdered Sugar**
Orange Powdered **Food Coloring**

Zip-Top Sandwich Bags, Large
Spoons, Large Mixing Bowl,
Small Crock Pot, Paper Plates

Advance Preparations:
On the day of the party:
▶ One hour before the party begins, place the margarine, peanut butter and chocolate chips in the small crock pot. Turn on low and heat until the chocolate chips melt. Stir frequently to keep it from burning.
▶ Stir the orange food coloring into the powdered sugar.

How To Make It:
1. Give each child a paper plate and a zip-top sandwich bag.
2. Pour the cereal into a large mixing bowl.
3. Pour the melted chocolate chip mixture over the cereal and mix with a large spoon until the cereal is well coated.
4. In small groups, have the children come to the table where a parent will place a large spoonful of colored powdered sugar and a few spoonfuls of cereal into their zip-top bag.
5. Next, the children will zip their bags closed and shake them until the cereal is coated with powdered sugar. Add additional powdered sugar if necessary.
6. Pour onto paper plates and enjoy!

MAKE AHEAD SPOOKTACULAR TREATS

Deviled Eyeballs, *Spicy Bat Wings*, *Toasted Bones* and *Halloween Sandwiches* — these ordinary foods have been given a special Halloween twist. Plenty of snack food ideas are also available in this section. *Cheesy Eyeballs*, *Roasted Pumpkin Seeds* and *Devils Snack Mix* are all great crowd pleasers. No party is complete without sinfully delicious desserts, so whip up an *Ooey Gooey Wormy Dessert*, a *Spider Ice Scream Pie*, a *Slithering Dessert* or a batch of *Mini Ghost Cookies* to satisfy your guest's sweet tooth.

IDEA #30

Cheesy Eyeballs *Pop these tasty*
eyeball appetizers out of the oven just before your guests
are ready to eat.

Recipe Will Make: About 20 Cheesy Eyeballs.

Supply List
2 cups grated **Cheddar Jack**
    Cheese w/Jalapeno Peppers
½ cup **Margarine**
1 teaspoon **Paprika**
1 cup **Flour**
20 **Black Olives**
    ———

Small Mixing Bowl, Spoon,
Knife, Cookie Sheet, Foil

How To Make Them:
1. Remove the margarine from the refrigerator to soften.
2. Preheat the oven to 400 degrees.
3. Line the cookie sheet with foil.
4. Cut each olive in half and drain on a paper towel.
5. In a small bowl, mix the grated cheese and softened margarine.
6. Slowly add the flour and paprika. The dough will be stiff but pliable.
7. Roll the dough into walnut size balls.
8. Use a spoon to hollow out a small section in the center of each piece of dough. Place an olive in the hole to make an 'eyeball' that is 'staring' outward.
9. Arrange the balls, olive side up, on the baking sheet. Space two inches apart.
10. Bake for approximately 15 minutes or until set.

Make Ahead Suggestion:
- If you want to make these ahead of time, place the UNBAKED 'eyeballs' in the freezer on the cookie sheet. When they are frozen, transfer them to a large plastic zip-top bag. On the day of the party, thaw and bake.

Deviled Eyeballs You will not have

to 'egg your guests on' to enjoy these deviled eyeballs.

Recipe Will Make: Two dozen Deviled Eyeballs.

Supply List

12 **Eggs**
24 **Green Olives** w/**Pimientos**
1 teaspoon **Mustard**
½ teaspoon **Salt**
¼ cup **Mayonnaise**
Red Gel Frosting

**Large Saucepan, Mixing Bowl,
Fork, Spoon, Paper Towels**

How To Make Them:

1. Remove olives from the jar and drain on a paper towel.
2. Place the eggs in a large saucepan and cover with cold water.
3. Bring to a boil and cook for 1 minute.
4. Remove from heat, cover, and let stand for 15 minutes.
5. Drain the hot water and run cold water over the eggs to prevent further cooking.
6. Peel the eggs. The easiest way to do this is to tap the egg a few times to crack the shell and then roll the egg between your hands to loosen the shell. Finally, hold the egg under cold running water to help ease off the shell.
7. Cut the eggs into halves.
8. Slice a small piece off the bottom of each half so the egg will sit flat on a plate.
9. Scoop out the yolks and put them in a mixing bowl.
10. Mash the yolks with a fork and add the mayonnaise, mustard and salt. Mix together until a smooth paste has formed.
11. Spoon the mixture back into the egg-white halves.
12. Place one olive in the middle of each yellow 'eyeball'.
13. Use the red gel to draw blood shots on each yellow 'eyeball'.
14. Cover and refrigerate for no more than 24 hours. (Be careful if covering with plastic wrap or foil, the red gel will stick to it.)

IDEA #32

Spicy Bat Wings Heat up your

*party with these spicy wings. To help put out the fire, serve
with Boo Cheese Dip and celery sticks.*

Recipe Will Make: About 48 Bat Wings.

Supply List

4 pounds of **Chicken Wings**
½ cup **Vinegar**
½ cup **Water**
4 tablespoons **Tomato Paste**
4 teaspoons **Sugar**
1-3 tablespoons (or to taste)
   Liquid Hot Pepper Seasoning
1-3 teaspoons (or to taste) ground
   Cayenne Red Pepper
Non-Stick Cooking Spray

2 bunches of **Celery (optional)**

**Small Bowl, Large Spoon, Knife,
2-10 x 15-inch Baking Pans**

How To Make Them:

1. Preheat oven to 400°.
2. Rinse the chicken wings.
3. Using a sharp knife, cut each chicken wing at the joints to make
   3 pieces. Discard the tip pieces. Cut off excess skin.
4. Spray the two baking pans with the non-stick cooking spray.
5. Arrange the chicken in the baking pans.
6. Bake for 30 minutes or until golden brown.
7. In a small bowl, make the hot pepper sauce by mixing together
   the vinegar, water, tomato paste, sugar, liquid hot pepper seasoning and cayenne pepper.
8. When the chicken is done, remove from the oven and drain off
   the fat.

IDEA #36

Roasted Pumpkin Seeds

While getting the seeds out of a pumpkin can be a slimy ordeal, munching on freshly toasted seeds is a real treat.

Recipe Will Make: Two cups of Pumpkin Seeds.

Supply List
2 cups **Pumpkin Seeds**
4 cups **Water**
2 tablespoons **Salt**
2 tablespoons **Margarine**
Non-Stick Cooking Spray
Optional **Seasonings**—Dry
    Packets of Ranch Dressing
    or Taco Seasoning

Small Saucepan, Strainer, Spoon, Cookie Sheet, Airtight Container, Paper Towels

How To Make It:
1. Preheat the oven to 350 degrees.
2. Spray the cookie sheet with the non-stick cooking spray.
3. Separate the pumpkin seeds from the pulp of the pumpkin and rinse well.
4. Place the pumpkin seeds, water and salt into the saucepan.
5. Simmer over low heat for 10 minutes.
6. Drain well in a strainer. Place on paper towels and pat dry.
7. Melt the margarine in the saucepan. Add the pumpkin seeds and slowly stir until evenly coated.
8. Spread the seeds evenly over the cookie sheet.
9. Bake for approximately 30 minutes, stirring occasionally. The seeds are ready when they are golden brown.
10. Sprinkle the seasoning over the pumpkin seeds and let cool.
11. Store in an airtight container.

Suggestion:
- To help separate the seeds from the pumpkin fiber, fill a bowl with water and let the pumpkin seeds soak for at least one hour.

Devils Snack Mix *This spicy snack will put some real zip into your Halloween Party.*

Recipe Will Make: About 11 cups of Devils Snack Mix.

Supply List

8 cups of **Corn, Rice or Wheat Cereal** (or any combination)
1 cup of hot and spicy **Peanuts**
1 cup of hot and spicy **Cheese Crackers**
1 cup of **Pretzels**
1 package of dry **Taco Seasoning Mix** (1.25 oz.)
6 tablespoons **Margarine**
1 tablespoon of **Worcestershire Sauce**
1 teaspoon of **Hot Pepper Sauce**

Roasting Pan, Spoon, Paper Towels, Airtight Container

How To Make It:

1. Preheat the oven to 250 degrees.
2. Place the margarine in a large roasting pan and melt in the oven.
3. Stir in the taco seasoning mix, worcestershire sauce and hot pepper sauce. Add one or two additional teaspoons of hot pepper sauce if you want to really spice it up!
4. Gradually stir in the remaining ingredients.
5. Bake for 1 hour, stirring every 15 minutes.
6. Spread the mixture on paper towels to cool.
7. Store in an airtight container until ready to serve.

Halloween Popcorn Balls

Candy corn and orange food coloring turn these popcorn balls into a colorful Halloween treat!

Recipe Will Make: About 24 Halloween Popcorn Balls.

Supply List

1½ cups **Sugar**
¾ cup **Margarine**
1½ cups light **Corn Syrup**
¾ teaspoon **Salt**
20 cups popped **Popcorn**
4 cups **Candy Corn**
Orange Food Coloring

Dutch Oven or **Roaster, Large Spoon, Wax Paper, Plastic Wrap** or **Bags**

How To Make Them:

1. Combine the sugar, margarine, corn syrup and salt in a dutch oven.
2. Place over medium high heat and bring to a boil while stirring constantly. Boil and stir for 2 **more** minutes. Remove from heat.
3. Add orange food coloring to the mixture until it is bright orange.
4. Stir in the popcorn and candy corn until well coated.
5. Cool slightly.
6. Dip hands in cold water.
7. Shape the mixture into balls about 4 inches in diameter.
8. Cool on wax paper.
9. Wrap balls individually in plastic wrap or place in plastic bags and seal.

Suggestion:

• Because the heated mixture is so hot, we suggest that only adults form the popcorn balls.

Ooey Gooey Wormy Dessert

Kids really enjoy "fishing" out the gummy worms in this easy-to-make dessert.

Recipe Will Make: About 8 servings.

Supply List

1 package of **Orange Gelatin**
   (large 8 serving size)
3 cups of **Water**
1 large package of **Gummy Worms**
Chocolate Sprinkles
Non-Stick Cooking Spray
___

Small Saucepan, Spoon, Knife, 9-inch Pie Plate, Serving Plate

How To Make It:

1. Spray the pie plate with non-stick cooking spray.
2. Boil 1½ cups of water in a small saucepan and remove from heat.
3. Pour the gelatin into the boiling water and stir 2 minutes, or until the gelatin is completely dissolved.
4. Add 1½ cups of **cold** water to the gelatin mixture.
5. Pour the gelatin into the pie plate.
6. Refrigerate for 45 minutes.
7. Remove from the refrigerator and push the gummy worms into the thickened gelatin.
8. Refrigerate for 2 additional hours or until firm.
9. Just before serving, add the chocolate sprinkles over the top of the gelatin until it resembles dirt.
10. Garnish with additional gummy worms.

IDEA #40

Spider's Ice Scream Pie *This colorful dessert will have your guests screaming for more.*

Recipe Will Make: One 9-inch Spider's Ice Scream Pie.

Supply List
1¼ cups **Chocolate Graham Crackers**
1/4 cup **Sugar**
1/3 cup **Margarine**
3/4 cup **Chocolate Fudge Sauce**
3 cups **Orange Sherbet**
1/2 cup **Mini Chocolate Chips**

Small Bowl, Medium Bowl, Spoon, Zip-Top Bag, Rubber Spatula, 9-inch Pie Plate

How To Make It:

1. Place the chocolate graham crackers in the zip-top bag, seal and crush into small crumbs.
2. In a small bowl, melt the margarine in the microwave.
3. Add the graham crackers and sugar to the margarine. Mix well.
4. Using a large spoon, press the crumb mixture onto the bottom and up the sides of the pie plate.
5. Place the crust in the freezer for 5 to 10 minutes.
6. Remove the crust from the freezer. With a rubber spatula, spread the chocolate fudge sauce evenly over the pie crust.
7. Place in the freezer to harden.
8. Remove the sherbet from the freezer to soften.
9. In a medium bowl, stir together the sherbet and chocolate chips.
10. Remove the crust from the freezer.
11. Spoon the sherbet mixture over the crust and smooth the top.
12. Return to the freezer until ready to serve.
13. Just before serving, place the extra fudge sauce in a zip-top bag, cut off the tip of a corner, and slowly squeeze a spiral of fudge over the top of the pie. With the tip of a spatula **quickly** make lines from the center to the outer edge (like the spokes of a wheel) to make it look like a spider's web.

IDEA #41

Mini Ghost Cookies
Ghouls and goblins of all ages enjoy making these easy treats.

Recipe Will Make: 16 Mini Ghost Cookies.

Supply List

16 **Nutter Butter®** Cookies
1 pkg. **Vanilla Almond Bark**
1 pkg. **Mini Chocolate Chips**

Small Saucepan, Large Spoon, Tongs, Wax Paper, Cookie Sheet

How To Make Them:
1. Cover cookie sheet with wax paper.
2. Place half of the almond bark in a saucepan.
3. Melt over very low heat for 8 minutes, stirring constantly until melted and smooth. (Check the melting directions on the package of almond bark since cooking times may vary.)
4. With the tongs, carefully drop each cookie in the melted almond bark, turn until covered and then remove from the pan. Shake lightly to remove excess coating and place on the wax paper.
5. Before the almond bark hardens completely, place two mini chocolate chips on each cookie to make eyes. If you wait too long you might have to 'glue' them on with a dab of frosting.

Suggestions:
- Do NOT overheat the almond bark. Overheating can cause it to scorch or caramelize. If this happens, pour it out and start over.
- If the almond bark seems too thick for dipping, add one tablespoon or more of **solid** vegetable shortening and stir until smooth.
- Other treats that can be dipped in the almond bark include pretzels, raisins, licorice and nuts.

Ice Scream Sandwiches *These*
make-ahead party treats are sure to please.

Recipe Will Make: About 8 Ice Scream Sandwiches.

Supply List
2-20 oz packages of refrigerated
  Sugar Cookie Dough
Halloween **Sprinkles**
½ gallon block of **Ice Cream**
LARGE Halloween **Cookie**
  Cutters

**Plastic Wrap, Cookie Sheets,
Large Knife, Spatula, Spoon**

How To Make Them:
1. Prepare the cookie dough as directed on the package.
2. Use the cookie cutters to cut out the cookies from the dough. You will need two of the same cookie shapes for each ice cream sandwich.
3. Decorate half of the cookies with the candy sprinkles. Help the sprinkles stay on by using your fingers to lightly press them into the dough.
4. Bake as directed on the package.
5. Remove the ice cream from the freezer. Use a large knife to cut a 3/4 inch slice off the block of ice cream.
6. Using the same cookie cutters, **quickly** cut the ice cream into shapes.
7. Place the ice cream between the cookies and wrap in plastic wrap.
8. Store in the freezer until ready to serve.

Suggestion:
- You can make this a fun activity at your party by letting the children make their own ice scream sandwiches. Bake the cookies ahead of time and have the ice cream and cookie cutters ready to use. Let the children cut out their cookie shapes from the ice cream and then make their own sandwich.

Slithering Dessert Let the little

ghouls and goblins at your party make their own delightfully wormy treat.

Recipe Will Make: 8-10 servings of Slithering Dessert.

Supply List
1 small package of **Orange Gelatin**
1 small package of **Grape Gelatin**
1¼ cups **Boiling Water**
1 envelope **Dream Whip**® **Whipped Topping Mix**
½ cup cold **Milk**
½ teaspoon **Vanilla**
30 **Straws**

Medium Mixing Bowl, Glass or **Container** (very tall and narrow), **Electric Mixer, Large Spoon**

How To Make It:
1. Pour the boiling water into the mixing bowl.
2. Add the two packets of gelatin.
3. Stir the mixture at least 3 minutes or until completely dissolved.
4. Pour the gelatin mixture into the tall container.
5. Place the straws in the container and push them to the bottom. (They should all be filled with gelatin.)
6. Place in the refrigerator for 3 hours or until firm to the touch.
7. Just before the party, prepare the Dream Whip® according to the directions on the box.
8. To remove the straws, carefully twist each straw individually and place on a plate. The gelatin should remain in each straw.
9. To serve, let the children put a spoonful of Dream Whip® on their plate and give them three gelatin-filled straws. They will then squeeze the straws to make their worms come out onto the whipped topping. Yuck!

Spider Web Brownies For
those guests who need a chocolate fix, serve these easy
brownies with a fun Halloween twist.

Recipe Will Make: Approximately 20 - 2½"x 3" Brownies.

Supply List
1 **Brownie Mix** (Family Size)
1 **Baking Pan** (13"x 9")
¼ cup **Powdered Sugar**
1 small mesh **Strainer**

***

Bowl, Large Spoon, Scissors,
Paint Brush, Razor Blade

How To Make Them:
1. Make a copy of the spider web pattern in Figure 7. You will need to enlarge the pattern by 50 percent to make it fit in a 13"x 9" pan.
2. With a razor blade, carefully cut out the spider web and spider.
3. Mix and bake the brownies according to the directions on the package.
4. Let them cool completely.
5. Place the paper spider web and spider stencils on top of the brownies.
6. While holding the strainer over the stencils, slowly pour some powdered sugar into the mesh strainer. Carefully tap the strainer with your hand to shake the sugar evenly over the stencils. Continue adding powdered sugar until the stencils are covered.
7. Carefully lift the stencils straight up and away from the brownies. It is helpful to have someone assist you with this step.
8. Use a clean paint brush to 'clean up' any powdered sugar that fell on your spider or web as you removed the stencil. Dipping the brush in water will help remove the sugar.
9. Cut into pieces after your guests have arrived.

Enlarge 50%

Figure 7: Stencil pattern for Spider Web Brownies.

SPOOKTACULAR BREWS AND OTHER IDEAS

As your party heats up, your guests will want to quench their horrific thirsts with one of our spooktacular brews. You can choose from cool and fruity beverages like *Witches Brew*, *Vampire Blood Smoothies* and *Vampire Punch*. For an adults only beverage that will warm your guest's spirits, try the *Boil & Bubble Brew*.

To add a special Halloween touch to your brews, serve them in a *Pumpkin Punch Bowl* or a *Boiling Caldron*— or float some *Spooktacular Ice Cubes* or *Frozen Zombie Hands* in your beverages.

IDEA #45

Witches Brew *Ghost and goblins of all ages will enjoy this delicious concoction.*

Recipe Will Make: 20-30 servings of Witches Brew.

Supply List

1 quart **Apple Cider**
1½ cups **Orange Juice**
1 cup **Pineapple Juice**
1 quart **Lemon Lime Soda Pop**
2 tablespoons **Sugar**
1 jar **Maraschino Cherries**
6-8 small **Oranges**
Cloves

**Large Punch Bowl, Ladle,
Paper Cups, Knife**

Advance Preparations:
On the day of the party:
- ▶ Wash the oranges.
- ▶ Use the cloves to make faces on the oranges.
- ▶ Cut the maraschino cherries in half. These will look like red eyeballs floating in the punch.
- ▶ Chill all of the juices and the soda pop.

How To Make It:
1. Mix the apple cider, orange juice, pineapple juice and the sugar together in a large punch bowl.
2. Stir in the lemon lime soda pop.
3. Add the oranges and maraschino cherries.
4. Pour into cups and it's ready to serve.

IDEA #46

Vampire Blood Smoothies

Make sure you whip up plenty of this tasty brew—your guests are sure to suck up seconds.

Recipe Will Make: 15-20 servings of Vampire Blood Smoothies

Supply List

1—large package frozen **Strawberries**
½ gallon **Strawberry Ice Cream**
1—2-liter bottle **Strawberry Soda Pop**
Red Sugar (optional)

Ice Cream Scoop, Blender, Glasses, Small Bowl

Advance Preparations:

▶ Thaw the strawberries in a bowl in your refrigerator.

How To Make It:

1. Pour 1/3 of the strawberries into the blender.
2. Add three scoops of ice cream to the strawberries.
3. Pour strawberry soda pop over the ice cream until the blender is 2/3 full.
4. Blend.
5. Add additional ice cream or soda pop until it is the consistency of a smoothie.
6. For a special touch, prepare the glasses for the smoothies by frosting the rims with red sugar. Simply dip the rims of the glasses in water and then into the red sugar.
7. Pour the smoothies into glasses and serve.

IDEA #47

Kiddie Brew *The floating eyeballs and gummy worms will make this a delightfully nasty brew.*

Recipe Will Make: 10-15 servings of Kiddie Brew.

Supply List
1—2-liter bottle **Root Beer**
½ gallon **Vanilla Ice Cream**
Root Beer Candies
Gummy Worms
1 tube **Red Gel Frosting**

Ice Cream Scoop, Aluminum Foil, Cookie Sheet, Ladle, Large Punch Bowl, Paper Cups

Advance Preparations:
► Line a cookie sheet (make sure it will fit in your freezer) with aluminum foil.
► With an ice cream scoop, place large scoops of ice cream onto the cookie sheet. These are suppose to look like 'eyeballs', so make them as round as possible.
► Press one piece of root beer candy into the middle of each 'eyeball' for the pupil.
► Place the 'eyeballs' in the freezer. If you are making them a day or more in advance, cover with plastic wrap.

How To Make It:
1. Remove the 'eyeballs' from the freezer. With the red gel frosting, draw blood veins radiating out from the candy pupils.
2. Pour the root beer into the punch bowl.
3. Carefully place the 'eyeballs' in the root beer so they are 'looking' at your guests.
4. Add the gummy worms.
5. Use a ladle to pour 'eyeballs' and root beer into paper cups.

Suggestion:
• Substitute orange soda pop for the root beer.

IDEA #48

Vampire Punch *Your guests will enjoy quenching their thirsts with this delicious punch.*

Recipe Will Make: 30-35 servings of Vampire Punch.

Supply List

1 (46 oz) can **Red Fruit Punch**
1 (6 oz) can frozen **Lemonade Concentrate**
1 (6 oz) can frozen **Orange Juice Concentrate**
1 (6 oz) can frozen **Grape Juice Concentrate**
3½ cups **Lemon Lime Soda Pop**
6 cups cold **Water**
Ice
1 jar **Maraschino Cherries**
5 small **Oranges**

Large Punch Bowl, Ladle, Clear Plastic Cups, Knife

Advance Preparations:
On the day of the party:
► Wash the oranges and cut into thin slices. These can be used as garnishes for the cups or float a few slices in the punch.
► One hour before the party, take the frozen juices out of the freezer. They should be thawed by party time.

How To Make It:
1. In the large punch bowl, combine the punch and thawed juices with the water.
2. Just before serving, add the soda pop and ice. Some orange slices may be added.
3. Pour into cups and garnish with an orange slice and a cherry.

IDEA #49

Black Magic Punch *When your devilish guests need to cool down, serve them this colorful punch.*

Recipe Will Make: 32 - ½ cup servings of Black Magic Punch.

Supply List

2—2-liter bottles **Orange Soda Pop**
1 pint **Blackberry Sherbet**
1 pint **Orange Sherbet**

Large Punch Bowl, Ice Cream Scoop, Ladle, Plastic Cups

Advance Preparations:

▶ Refrigerate the soda pop.

How To Make It:

1. Pour the orange soda into a large punch bowl.
2. With the ice cream scoop, add small round portions of black-berry and orange sherbet to the orange soda pop.
3. To serve, ladle the punch into plastic cups.

Helpful Hint

To make clear ice cubes, boil the water before you put it in the freezer.

IDEA #50

Boil & Bubble Brew *Concoct*

this robust brew for your ghoulish adult guests, or omit the wine and serve to the little goblins, too.

Recipe Will Make: 32 - ½ cup servings of Boil & Bubble Brew.

Supply List

10 cups **Apple Cider**
6 cups dry **Red Wine** (substitue apple cider for non-alcoholic)
½ cup packed **Brown Sugar**
2 teaspoons whole **Cloves**
2 teaspoons whole **Allspice**
2 sticks of **Cinnamon**

3 small **Oranges**
Cloves
Cinnamon Sticks

Large Stock Pot, Ladle, Cups, Knives

How To Make It:

1. Combine the wine, apple cider, brown sugar, allspice, cloves and cinnamon sticks in a large stock pot.
2. Bring to a boil.
3. Reduce the heat, cover and simmer for 20 minutes.
4. Reduce heat to low to keep warm.
5. Wash the oranges well.
6. Slice the oranges in half.
7. With the cloves, make pumpkin faces on the oranges.
8. Place the clove studded orange slices in the pot.
9. Ladle the brew into cups and garnish with a cinnamon stick.

IDEA #51

Pumpkin Punch Bowl

To keep with the Halloween spirit, serve any cold brew in a fun pumpkin punch bowl.

Supply List

1 large **Pumpkin**	**Aluminum Foil**
Black Acrylic Paint	**Paint Brush**

Knife, Scoop, Newspapers

How To Make It:
1. Hollow out a large pumpkin.
2. Line the inside of the pumpkin with aluminum foil.
3. Paint a face on the pumpkin and let dry.
4. Refrigerate.
5. Carefully pour the cold drink of your choice into the pumpkin and serve.

IDEA #52

Spooktacular Ice Cubes

Your guests will get a real startling treat in their drinks when you serve them with these creepy-crawly ice cubes.

Supply List

Gummy Worms
Candy Bugs
Water or **Flavored Beverage**
Ice Cube Trays

How To Make Them:
1. Fill the ice cube trays with water or a flavored beverage.
2. Add a gummy worm or candy bug to each ice cube.
3. Freeze until solid.
4. Place the ice cubes in your punch bowl or in your guest's cups.

Boiling Caldron *It is easy to turn*
any cold beverage into a spooktacular drink by serving it
in a caldron that looks like it is boiling over.

Supply List

Dry Ice
Hot Water
Large **Metal Bowl**
Large **Black Plastic Caldron**

Pitcher, Heavy Work Gloves,
Hammer

How To Make It:

1. Place the metal bowl in the bottom of a large black plastic caldron. The container you are going to put your punch or drink in
   should fit inside the large metal bowl. There needs to be enough
   space for the 'fog' to encircle the drink container.
2. Read the safety instructions on the dry ice package. **Always**
   handle the dry ice with care and wear gloves at all times. If
   the dry ice comes in contact with bare skin, an injury similar to a
   burn will result. Use dry ice only in a well ventilated area.
3. On a hard concrete surface, break the dry ice into 6 inch pieces
   with a hammer. Place ice back in its original package and store
   in the freezer until party time.
4. When you are ready to serve your beverage, fill the metal bowl
   half full with HOT water.
5. Place the metal bowl inside the plastic caldron.
6. With gloves, remove a piece of dry ice from the freezer and
   carefully place it in the hot water.
7. Place your beverage container inside the metal bowl. The 'fog'
   should now be rolling over the sides of the caldron.
8. When the 'fog' begins to dissipate, add another piece of dry ice
   and pour more hot water into the metal bowl.

CAUTION: Do not let children play in the caldron, they could get
burned!

IDEA #54

Frozen Zombie Hands *Keep*

your Halloween brews cold with these chilling hands.

Supply List

2 **Plastic** or **Latex Gloves**
1 package **Drink Mix** (like Kool Aid®)
1 cup **Sugar** (check drink mix)
2 **Twist-Ties**

———

Pitcher, Paper Towels, Cookie Sheet, Freezer, Scissors

How To Make Them:

1. Wash the gloves. If they have a powdery residue inside, turn them inside out and wash well with soapy water. Rinse well and let dry.
2. Line the cookie sheet with paper towels.
3. In a pitcher, mix together the drink mix and sugar. Stir until the sugar is completely dissolved.
4. Carefully pour the drink into the gloves. Add enough to fill the gloves, but not so full that the fingers can't move.
5. Seal the gloves tightly with twist-ties.
6. Carefully lay the 'hands' on the cookie sheet.
7. Place the cookie sheet in the freezer and allow to freeze until solid (overnight).
8. When you are ready to serve your drink, take the 'hands' out of the freezer and carefully use scissors to cut the gloves off of the 'hands'.
9. Place the 'hands' in the punch bowl where they will float and keep the drink cool.

Suggestions:

- Choose a flavor of drink mix that will taste good when combined with the brew you are serving.
- Choose a drink mix that contrasts with the color of the brew you are serving. If necessary, use food coloring to change the original color of the drink mix.

SPOOKTACULAR RELAY GAMES

When your guests begin to get restless and need to run off some energy, try some of the relay games in this section. To avoid accidents, make sure the game area is clear of all furniture and breakable or sharp objects.

Choose the relay games that are appropriate for the ages of your guests and always divide them into teams that are as even as possible. Plan on playing each game at least twice— your guests will get better each time they play! Keep score and award everyone a prize when the games are complete.

Have a great time!

IDEA #55

Pass The Pumpkin *Children of all ages will enjoy playing this fast paced relay game over and over again.*

Suggested Age: Preschool—Adult

Object Of The Game: To be the first team to get the pumpkin back to the leader.

Supply List

Unbreakable Pumpkin — one for each team
Suggestion: Use pumpkin buckets or pumpkins made of foam or rubber.

How To Play:

1. Divide your guests into teams.
2. Pick one leader for each team.
3. Have the players line up behind their team leader.
4. Explain the object of the game. Demonstrate how the pumpkins will be passed down the row (see below). An important rule is that all the players must stay in line.
5. On the signal "Go", each team will pass the pumpkin down the row and back to the leader.
6. The first team to finish wins the relay.
7. Keep a running tally of which team wins and play again, but this time pass the pumpkin a different way.

Ways To Pass The Pumpkin:
1. Over the head.
2. Through the legs.
3. Back to back.
4. Elbows only.
5. One handed.
6. Sitting on the floor facing forward.
7. Over the first player, through the legs of the second player, over the third player, etc.

Follow The Ghost Relay

Children young and old really enjoy the mystery associated with this simple game. The ghosts will 'tell' each guest what they must do.

Suggested Age: 2nd Grade—Adult

Object Of The Game: Race to one end of the room, pick a ghost and return to the line while following the instruction written on the ghost. The first team to finish the race wins.

Supply List

Ghost Suckers (see page 118) - 1 for each guest
Chairs - 1 for each team
Halloween Sacks - 1 for each team

———

Paper, Scissors, Tape

Advance Preparations:
► Make one ghost sucker for each guest.
► Think of some things to do such as jump, crawl, hop, skip, (front wards or backwards) etc. Write the activities on a small strip of paper and tape to the stick of each ghost. Make sure each team does the same activities and store in the Halloween sacks.

On the day of the party:
► Set up the race area so the furniture is out of the way.
► Place the chairs at the far end of the room and put a sack of ghost suckers on each chair.

How To Play:
1. Divide your guests into teams and line them up in straight lines.
2. Explain the object of the game. Demonstrate if necessary.
3. On the signal "GO", the first player on each team runs to the chair and picks a ghost sucker from the sack. The player then hurries back to their line, following the instruction on the ghost, and 'tags' the next person.
4. Play continues until everyone has had a turn.
5. The team that finishes first wins.

IDEA #57

Eyeball Dig Relay *Children of all ages will enjoy digging through the black gelatin to find buried prizes.*

Suggested Age: Preschool—5th Grade

Object Of The Game: To be the first team to successfully find all of their prizes.

Supply List

Prepared **Black Gelatin** (Orange and Grape Gelatin)
3 **Spooky Prizes** per child (rubber spiders, snakes, eyeballs, vampire fangs, bouncing balls, etc.)
Plastic **Sandwich Bags**—one for each child
1 **Bell**
1 very large **Container**
Newspapers
Paper Towels

Advance Preparations:

▶ Prepare the gelatin in large containers according to the directions on the package. To make black gelatin, mix equal amounts of grape and orange gelatin together. When slightly thick, add the spooky prizes to the gelatin. **Note:** Adjust the number of packages of gelatin that you make according to the number of children that will be playing the game. If a large number of children will be attending the party, divide the prizes between a few parents and have each of them make a large batch of the gelatin.

On the day of the party:

▶ Set up the area where the 'digging' will take place by covering the floor and table top with newspapers. If there is a sink in the room, place this game near the sink for easier clean up.

► Pour all of the gelatins into one very large container.
► Place the bell, paper towels, and plastic sandwich bags on a table near the sink.

How To Play:

1. Divide the children into two teams.
2. Have each team line up in front of the large gelatin container and sit down. Those children wearing long sleeves will need to roll them up.
3. Explain the object of the game. Demonstrate how they will dig for their prizes and then go to the clean up area when finished.
4. On the signal "GO", the first child in each line will do the following:
   A. Go to the large container and get on their knees.
   B. Close their eyes.
   C. Dig until they find their prizes (one of each).
   D. Open their eyes.
   E. Stand up, go to the clean up area and ring the bell.
5. When the bell rings, that is the signal for the next child in line to start digging. Meanwhile, the child who just finished digging will need to put the prizes in a plastic sandwich bag, wash up, and sit down at the end of the line.
6. Play continues until everyone has had a turn.

Helpful Hint

This game can get rather messy. You might want to have old shirts available for the children to wear while they are digging in the gelatin.

IDEA #58

Evil Twin Relay *Have you ever wondered what it would be like to be a Siamese Twin? This game 'sticks' two guests together and the results are quite amusing!*

Suggested Age: 3rd Grade—Adult

Object Of The Game: To be the first team to retrieve all of the objects from their bucket.

```
                      Supply List

  2 Buckets
  1 Halloween Prize for each guest (skeletons,
       plastic spiders, eyeballs, rings, etc.)
  2 Chairs
  Masking Tape
```

Advance Preparations:
On the day of the party:
▶ In an area that has been cleared of all furniture, lay out the course. With the masking tape, mark the two starting lines. Place the chairs at the opposite end of the room.
▶ Divide the Halloween prizes evenly and put in the buckets.
▶ Place the buckets on the chairs.

How To Play:
1. Divide your guests into two teams. If there is an odd number of guests on a team, have one player go twice.
2. The Siamese Twins are formed by having two players stand back-to-back while linking their arms at the elbows. Have two guests demonstrate before the race begins. **Their arms must stay linked at all times!** Have them try to walk together. The easiest way to walk straight is to have one player walk forward while his/her partner walks backwards.
3. Have the guests pair up with someone on their team. This will be their 'Siamese Twin'.

4. Have the teams form two lines behind the starting line.
5. On the signal "GO", the first set of 'Siamese Twins' will walk to the bucket.
6. When they reach the bucket, **each player** will take one treat out of the bucket and then return to the starting line. (Their arms must remain linked at all times.)
7. As soon as the first set crosses the starting line, the second set of 'Siamese Twins' should head for the bucket.
8. Continue playing until all of your guests have retrieved a prize from the bucket.
9. The first team to finish wins.

Suggestions:

*   Be sure to allow plenty of time for this race. It is not as easy as it may seem.
*   Children often like to play this game a number of times. They get better at working together each time they play.
*   Because of the amount of coordination that is required to play this game, it is suggested that young children not participate in this relay.

Helpful Hint

Have all the children practice walking with their twin before the race begins. The results are hilarious and a lot of fun!

Witch Drawing Relay *Be prepared. This game is so much fun the children will want to play it over and over again!*

Suggested Age: 1st Grade—7th Grade

Object Of The Game: To be the first team to draw all of the parts of a witch.

Supply List

2 large sheets of **Paper**
Index Cards
2 **Crayons**
Masking Tape

Advance Preparations:

▶ Draw the outline of a witch on each piece of paper.
▶ On the index cards, write things that can be drawn on the witch— eyes, nose, wart, hat, dress, shoes, belt, etc. Be sure to have one card for each child.

On the day of the party:

▶ Clear the relay area of all furniture.
▶ Tape two sheets of paper to a wall or door at one end of the room.
▶ Place the index cards and crayons on the floor under each sheet of paper.

How To Play:

1. Divide the children into two teams. Have the children form two straight lines across the room from the papers.
2. Explain the object of the game.
3. On the signal "GO", the first child in each line will WALK to the picture, choose an index card and draw that item. The child then returns to their team, gives the crayon to the next child in line, and sits down at the end of the line.
4. The next child in line takes a turn drawing something on the witch.
5. Play continues until everyone has had a turn drawing on the witch.

IDEA #60

Winter Costume Relay No

matter what their ages, all of your guests will enjoy participating in this relay game.

Suggested Age: Preschool—Adult

Object Of The Game: To be the first team to have all of their members dress and undress.

Supply List

2 **Clothes Baskets**
2 complete outfits of **Winter Clothing**

Advance Preparations:

▶ Gather together two sets of winter clothing and place in the clothes baskets. Examples of items that work well include large winter coats, snow boots, stocking hats, scarves and a large pair of gloves. Make sure each team has the same outfits.

On the day of the party:

▶ Clear the relay area of all furniture.
▶ Place the two clothes baskets at the far end of the room.

How To Play:

1. Divide the children into two teams. Have the children form two straight lines across the room from the clothes baskets.
2. Explain the object of the game.
3. On the signal "GO", the first person in each line will go to the clothes basket, put on all of the clothing items and race back to their team. The clothes are then removed and passed on to the next person in line. The second person dresses in the clothes, runs to the clothes basket, removes the clothes, runs back to their team and 'tags' the next person in line.
4. This clothing exchange continues until each guest has had a turn.
5. The first team to finish wins.

IDEA #61

Suck It Up Relay *Be careful not*
to make your teammates laugh...it could cost you the game.

Suggested Age: Kindergarten—Adult

Object Of The Game: To be the first team to fill their container with ghosts without using their hands.

Supply List

1 **Ghost Eraser** for each guest
1 **Drinking Straw** for each guest
2 **Halloween Buckets** or **Containers**
2 **Chairs**

Advance Preparations:
On the day of the party:
▶ Clear the relay area of all furniture.
▶ Place the two chairs at the far end of the room.
▶ Place the two empty Halloween containers on the chairs.

How To Play:
1. Divide your guests into two teams and line them up in straight lines.
2. Give each guest a straw and a ghost eraser.
3. Explain the object of the game. Demonstrate how to hold the ghost on their straw without using their hands. If a ghost drops on the floor, they can only use their straw, NOT their hands, to pick it up.
4. The first person in each line places the straw in their mouth and sucks in so that the ghost eraser sticks to the end of the straw. While continuing to suck in, they will quickly WALK to the chair on the other side of the room and drop their ghost into the container. They will then turn around, run back to the line and 'tag' the next person in line.
5. Play continues until everyone has dropped their ghost into the containers.

IDEA #62

Pass The Kiss Relay *This simple game provides lots of fun and excitement for guests young and old.*

Suggested Age: Kindergarten—Adult

Object Of The Game: To be the first team to unwrap all of their candy.

Supply List

Wrapped Halloween Candy (like Hersheys Kisses®)
2 pairs of large **Gloves**
2 **Halloween Containers**

Advance Preparations:
▶ Divide the candy in half and place in the Halloween containers. Have extra candy on hand in case your guests want to play this game again.

How To Play:
1. Divide your guests into two teams.
2. In an area that has been cleared of all furniture, have the teams sit in a straight line, one behind the other, on the floor.
3. Explain the object of the game.
4. Give the first person in each line the container with the candy and a pair of gloves.
5. On the signal "GO", the first person on each team will put on the gloves and unwrap one piece of candy.
6. When they are done, they will quickly remove the gloves and pass the candy container and gloves to the next person in line.
7. The game continues until everyone has unwrapped a piece of candy.

Suggestion:
• Use small mittens or gloves for younger children and oversized work gloves for older children and adults.

IDEA #63

 Candy Corn Relay *Concentration and coordination is the secret to winning this game.*

Suggested Age: Preschool—Adult

Object Of The Game: To be the first team to transfer all of their candy corn from one container to another.

Supply List

2 **Large Spoons**—one for each team
2 bags of **Candy Corn**
4 **Halloween Containers**—2 for each team
4 **Chairs**

Advance Preparations:
On the day of the party:
▶ Set up two chairs per team at opposite ends of the room.
▶ Pour the candy corn into two containers and place on the chairs at the far end of the room. Place the two empty containers on the other two chairs.

How To Play:
1. Divide your guests into two teams. Have them line up behind the chairs with the empty containers.
2. Explain the object of the game.
3. Give the first person on each team a large spoon.
4. On the signal "GO", they will WALK to the chair at the other end of the room, scoop up some candy corn, and using only one hand to hold the spoon (younger children can use two hands), WALK to the empty container and pour out the candy corn. They will then hand the spoon to the next person in line.
5. Play continues until one team has transferred all of their candy corn from one container to the next.

Variation:
• The team that drops the fewest pieces of candy corn will be the winner. If neither team drops any pieces, then the team that finishes first wins.

IDEA #64

Pass It Fast Relay *You never know what is coming next in this fast paced relay game.*

Suggested Age: Preschool—5th Grade

Object Of The Game: To be the first team to pass all of the objects down their line and back.

Supply List

Each <u>team</u> will need the following objects:

Halloween Balloon	Cloth or Plastic Pumpkin
Sticky Eyeball	Plastic Mouse
Spider Ring	Rubber Finger
Bendable Skeleton	Gummy Worm
Chair	Halloween Sack

Advance Preparations:
On the day of the party:
▶ Set up two chairs at the far end of the room.
▶ Place one of each item in the Halloween sacks.

How To Play:
1. Divide the children into two teams. Have them form two lines.
2. Position one adult at the front of each line. They will be in charge of passing out the objects and telling the children when it is okay for the next item to be passed.
3. Explain the object of the game.
4. On the signal "GO", the first child in each line is handed an object. It is passed down the line until it reaches the chair. As soon as the object is placed on the chair, the next item is started.
5. When all the objects are on the chair, the last person in line begins passing them back, one at a time.
6. The first team to finish wins.

Variation:
• Have the children sit on the floor with their legs crossed and all facing the same direction. While they are passing the objects they are not allowed to turn around. This really takes team work.

IDEA #65

Ghostly Platter Relay *These ghosts have a mind of their own for this exciting relay.*

Suggested Age: Kindergarten—Adult

Object Of The Game: To be the first team to race around the chair and back while keeping the 'ghost' on their plate.

Supply List

White Balloons—1 for each guest   2 large **Trash Bags**
Paper Plates—1 for each guest   2 **Chairs**
Black Permanent Markers   **Masking Tape**

Advance Preparations:

▶ Blow up the balloons. Store in the large trash bags.
On the day of the party:
 ▶ Make a starting line on the floor with a long piece of tape.
 ▶ Place the 2 chairs at the opposite end of the room.

How To Play:

1. Give each of your guests a balloon and a paper plate.
2. With the black markers, have them draw a ghoulish face on their balloon.
3. Divide your guests into two teams and line them up in straight lines.
4. Explain the object of the game and demonstrate. If the balloon falls off of the plate, they must STOP, pick it up and continue.
5. On the signal "GO", the first person in each line will place their ghost on their plate, race around a chair and 'tag' the next person in line.
6. Play continues until everyone has had a turn.

Variation:

• To make this game more difficult, make them go back to the starting line if they drop their balloon.

IDE A #66

 Magical Stick Relay This
balloon race takes a lot of concentration and coordination.

Suggested Age: 2nd Grade—Adult

Object Of The Game: To hold a balloon with two sticks,
walk around a chair, and hand-off the balloon and sticks to the next
person in line.

Supply List

Each <u>team</u> will need:
- 2 **Black** or **Orange Balloons**
- 2 **Sticks** (rulers, chopsticks, paper towel tubes)
- 2 **Chairs**

Advance Preparations:
On the day of the party:
► Clear the relay area of all furniture.
► Place the chairs at the far end of the room. These will be the
turnaround points.
► Blow up the balloons. Each team will need one balloon. The
other balloon is an extra if one should pop.

How To Play:
1. Divide your guests into teams and line them up in straight lines.
2. Explain the object of the game. Demonstrate if necessary.
3. On the signal "GO", the first player on each team will hold the
balloon between the two sticks and quickly WALK around the
chair and back to the front of the line.
4. The balloon and sticks are then transferred to the next person in
line without touching the balloon. If a balloon is dropped, the
player who dropped it must use the sticks to pick it up.
5. The team that finishes first wins.

IDEA #67

Halloween Balloon Pop

This noisy relay game is always a big hit.

Suggested Age: Preschool—Adult

Object Of The Game: To be the first team to pop all of their balloons.

Supply List

Orange and **Black Balloons**—1 for each guest
2 large **Trash Bags**
2 **Chairs**

Advance Preparations:

▶ Blow up the balloons. Store in the large trash bags.
   On the day of the party:
   ▶ Clear the relay area of all furniture.
   ▶ Place the two chairs at the far end of the room.

How To Play:

1. Divide your guests into two teams. Position two 'helpers' at the starting line and have your guests form two lines behind them. Each of the 'helpers' will have a bag of balloons.
2. Explain the object of the game and demonstrate how they will pop their balloon.
3. On the signal "GO", the first person in each line will take a balloon, run to the chair at the opposite end of the room, and sit on the balloon until it pops. They will then return to their line, 'tag' the next person, and sit down at the end of the line.
4. After being 'tagged', the next person in line takes a turn at popping a balloon.
5. Play continues until everyone has popped a balloon.

Variation:

• To make this more difficult for older guests, give them a deflated balloon at the starting line. They must blow it up and tie it before running to the chair to pop it.

Back-To-Back Relay *Everyone must cooperate and work as a team to win this game.*

Suggested Age: 2nd Grade—Adult

Object Of The Game: To be the first team to place all of their balloons in their basket without using their hands.

Supply List

Orange and **Black Balloons**—1 for every 2 guests
2 large **Trash Bags**
2 **Laundry Baskets**

Advance Preparations:
▶ Blow up the balloons. Store in the large trash bags.
On the day of the party:
▶ Clear the relay area of all furniture.
▶ Place the two laundry baskets at the far end of the room.

How To Play:
1. Divide your guests into two teams. Everyone will then need to choose a partner from their own team.
2. Place the two bags of balloons at the starting line and have each team form a line behind the bags.
3. Explain the object of the game. Demonstrate how the two partners will stand back-to-back with the balloon between them. They are not allowed to use their hands. If the balloon drops, the pair must go back to the starting line and start over.
4. On the signal "GO", the first pair in each line will race to the laundry basket at the opposite end of the room and drop their balloon into the basket. They will then return to their team, 'tag' the next pair in line, and sit down.
5. Play continues until everyone has deposited their balloons in their laundry basket.

Mysterious Relay *The special directions in each balloon puts a frenzied twist into this noisy relay.*

Suggested Age: 3rd Grade—Adult

Object Of The Game: To be the first team to complete all the activities in their balloons.

> ## Supply List
>
> **Orange** and **Black Balloons**—1 for each guest
> 1 piece of **Paper**
> 2 large **Trash Bags**

Advance Preparations:
▶ Cut the piece of paper into small pieces (about 3"x 1/2").
▶ Think of some 'activity' (crawl backwards, ring the doorbell, eat some crackers and whistle, run up and down the stairs, etc.) and write it on two of the little pieces of paper. Place these slips of paper in separate stacks (1 stack for each team). Continue writing activities until you have one for each guest.
▶ Using one stack of activities at a time, put each slip of paper into a balloon, blow up and store in the large trash bags.

On the day of the party:
▶ Place the two bags of balloons at the opposite end of the room.

How To Play:
1. Divide your guests into two teams and line them up in straight lines.
2. Explain the object of the game and tell them they most pop a balloon and do the 'activity' inside it before returning to their line.
3. On the signal "GO", the first person in each line will run to the bag, pick a balloon, pop it, read the activity, do the activity and finally, 'tag' the next person in line.
4. Play continues until everyone has had a turn.

SPOOKTACULAR ACTIVE GAMES

Ghosts and goblins of all ages will enjoy the fun games in this section. Divide your guests into teams and have them compete against one another in the *Mummy Wrap Game*, the *Balloon Stuff Game* or the *Pass The Spider Race*. For a game that will test everyone's individual skill (and luck), play the *Suspended Apple Race*.

Scavenger hunts are always a lot of fun. You will find two types of hunts in this section. The *Halloween Scavenger Hunt* can be played in a classroom or at home, while the *Devilish Scavenger Hunt* will be done all around your town. Whichever you choose to play, your guests are guaranteed to have a wonderful time.

IDEA #70

Mummy Wrap Game It's easy
to get 'wrapped up' in this game! Team work is the secret
to success when playing this game.

Suggested Age: Kindergarten—Adult

Object Of The Game: To be the first team to wrap the
mummy up so that skin or clothing cannot be seen.

Supply List

Each <u>team</u> will need:
    2 rolls of **Toilet Paper**
    1 roll of **Tape**
    1 **Trash Bag**

How To Play:

1. Divide your guests into teams.
2. Each team will pick one person to be the Mummy. The other team
   members will be the wrappers.
3. Give each team two rolls of toilet paper and one roll of tape.
4. Explain to your guests that they are to completely wrap their
   Mummy from head to toe so that no clothing or skin can be seen,
   except for the Mummy's nose and mouth. These cannot be covered.
5. If the toilet paper breaks, they must repair it with tape. They are
   trying to wrap their Mummy with one continuous roll of toilet
   paper.
6. "Go!"
7. The team that finishes first wins.

Helpful Hint

Breaking out of the toilet paper is great fun, yet it can
create a mess. A fun second game is to see which
team can 'trash' their mummy wrap the quickest.

IDEA #71

Balloon Stuff Game *It is fun to watch your guests work as a team to win this race. The end of this game is as much fun as the game itself.*

Suggested Age: Kindergarten—Adult

Object Of The Game: To stuff as many balloons into each sweat suit as possible in one minute.

Supply List

Each **team** will need:

20-30 small **Balloons**	1 large **Trash Bag**
1 extra large **Sweat Shirt**	**Toothpicks**
1 extra large pair of **Sweat Pants**	**Watch**

Advance Preparations:

▶ Blow up the balloons and place half of them in each large trash bag.

How To Play:

1. Divide your guests into two groups.
2. Have the smallest person in each group put on the sweat suit.
3. Explain the object of the game.
4. On the signal "GO", the team members will begin to stuff the balloons into the sweat suit.
5. After one minute, shout "STOP" and your guests will stop stuffing the balloons. The team with the fewest balloons left wins.
6. If time permits, play again by carefully removing the balloons and putting them back in the trash bag. Count to make sure each team has an equal number of balloons. Choose another member of the team to 'get stuffed'.
7. After the last game has been played, determine the winner by counting the number of balloons that have been stuffed in the sweat suit. A fun way to do this is to hand out toothpicks to all of the 'stuffers'. Your guests will take turns popping the balloons with their toothpicks, one team at a time. Everyone can help count the pops!

IDEA #72

Suspended Apple Race It is

quite a sight to watch children and adults try to take a bite out of an apple that is suspended from a clothesline...it is also very difficult.

Suggested Age: 2nd Grade—Adult

Object Of The Game: To see who can be the first to take a bite out of their apple.

Supply List

Small **Apples**—1 for each guest
Large **Paper Sacks**
String—3´- 4´ for each guest
Clothesline or **Heavy Rope**
Large **Needle**

Advance Preparations:

▶ Cut the string into 3´ to 4´ lengths—one for each guest. The actual length will depend upon how tall your guests are and whether you will be suspending the apples from a clothesline or the ceiling.

▶ With the large needle and string, thread the string through the core of the apple and then back through the other side of the apple. See Figure 8. If your apples have stems and they seem to be secure, you can tie the strings onto them. There is a good chance the stems could fall off, so I recommend threading the string through the apple.

▶ Wrap the string around each apple so that it will not get tangled up with the other apples. Store in the paper sacks.

On the day of the party:

▶ Hang the clothesline across the room.

▶ Tie some of the apples to the clothesline. Because of the various heights of your guests, hang some of the apples lower than others. The strings can always be shortened by tying a knot in them.

How To Play:

1. Divide your guests into groups.
2. One group at a time, have each guest stand by an apple that is about shoulder high. Adjust the length of the string if necessary.
3. Explain the object of the game. One very important rule is that no one can use their hands, elbows, or shoulders to help hold the apple in place.
4. On the signal "GO", your guests will try to take a bite out of their apple.
5. The game is over when someone has taken a bite.
6. Give each guest the apple that they have been trying to bite.
7. Hang a new group of apples and continue playing until all of your guests have had a turn.
8. If time allows, have a 'Grand Champion' race among the winners of each game.

Suggestion:

• Have an apple corer, knives and some caramel or fruit dip available for your guests to dip their apples in.

Figure 8: How to suspend an apple by a string.

IDEA #73

Halloween Scavenger Hunt

Your guests will enjoy searching high and low for these special items.

Suggested Age: 2nd Grade—Teenagers

Object Of The Game: To find the objects that begin with each letter of the phrase 'HAUNTING ZOMBIES'. Bonus points are given to the team that finds the smallest object for each letter.

Supply List

Each team will need:
  1 piece of **Paper**   1 **Pencil**
  1 plastic **Halloween Container**

Piece of **Notebook Paper** (Score Pad)

Advance Preparations:

▶ Write the words HAUNTING ZOMBIES (you may choose another phrase) down the left hand side of each piece of paper. Place an X after the letters N and I in the word HAUNTING since these are duplicate letters. This will be the scavenger hunt list.

How To Play:

1. Divide your guests into groups of four and have them sit together.
2. Give each team a scavenger hunt list, a pencil, and a Halloween container.
3. Explain the object of the game. As they find an item, they need to write its name next to the proper letter and put it in their container. They will have 10 minutes to find as many objects as possible.
4. On the signal "GO", each team will begin to search the room for objects that begin with the letters on their scavenger hunt list.
5. When the time is up, have everyone sit down with their group.
6. Starting with the first letter on the list, 'H', have each team hold up the item they found that begins with 'H'. Give each team 1 point if they found an item that began with the letter 'H'. Award the team with the smallest item 2 extra points. Continue awarding points for each letter in the phrase.
7. The team with the most points wins.

IDEA #74

Flying Ghost Game *This fun-to-play numbers game can easily be adapted to a variety of grade levels.*

Suggested Age: 1st Grade—5th Grade

Object Of The Game: To be the person who 'collects' the most points.

Supply List

White Construction Paper
Black Marker
1 flat **Sheet** (twin or full)

Advance Preparations:
▶ Using the white construction paper, cut out various sizes of ghosts. Make at least five ghosts for each child.
▶ Write a number on each ghost. You can write large numbers on the small ghosts and small numbers on the large ghosts or you can be totally random with your numbers.

How To Play:
1. In an area that has been cleared of all furniture, have the children form a circle.
2. Explain the object of the game.
3. In the middle of the circle place the ghosts on top of the sheet.
4. Have two adults hold the corners of the sheet and toss the ghosts up in the air and let them fall to the floor.
5. On the signal "GO", have the children scramble to collect five ghosts.
6. After they have collected their ghosts, have them add their numbers together. The child with the most points wins.

Variations:
• Write addition, subtraction, multiplication or division facts on the ghosts for older children.

IDEA #75

Devilish Scavenger Hunt

Your party will be a sure hit with this video scavenger hunt. Watching the videos is as much fun as making them.

Suggested Age: Kindergarten—Adult

Object Of The Game: To video tape each team member doing the activities on the scavenger hunt list.

> ## Supply List
>
> Each <u>team</u> will need:
> | | |
> |---|---|
> | 1 **Video Camera** | 1 **Scavenger Hunt List** |
> | 1 **Car** | 1 **Pencil** or **Ink Pen** |
> | 1 **Watch** | |
>
> **Television, VCR, Score Pad**

Advance Preparations:
► Make copies of the scavenger hunt list on the following page or make up your own list.
► Make arrangements with guests to bring video cameras. You will need one for each team. Plan on four to five guests per team.

How To Play:
1. Divide your guests into groups of four to five people.
2. Hand out one scavenger hunt list to each team. Tell them **NOT** to look at it.
3. Explain that they are to video tape **EACH** member of their team doing **EACH** of the activities on the list. If the list says to do something as a group or together, they must follow that direction.
4. Tell them a specific time when everyone must return to your house.
5. Explain that this is **NOT** a race and everyone needs to be safe, obey the laws, and have fun! "GO".
6. After everyone has returned, have each team rewind their video tapes to the beginning. Plug the video camera into your VCR and enjoy the videos. You can keep score if you like.

SPOOK–TACULAR SCAVENGER HUNT

<u>Everyone</u> must do the following activities:

- Pet a horse and all <u>together</u> sing the 'Old McDonald' song.
- Skip a rock on a pond.
- <u>Individually</u> run around the bases on a baseball field and <u>together</u> at home plate sing 'Take Me Out To The Ball Game'.
- Video tape everyone <u>together</u> in a Port-A-Potty.
- At a car lot, find a convertible and have one person try to 'sell' it to the others in the group.
- Find a Halloween movie at the video store and <u>individually</u> tell the camera if you have seen it and if you liked it.
- Go down a slide. <u>Everyone must go down a different way</u>.
- In front of an ice cream store, everyone <u>together</u> must say:
  "I Scream, You Scream, We All Scream For Ice Cream."
- Find the entrance to a graveyard and tape <u>everyone</u> standing around the sign that tells the name of the cemetery.
- Salute a flag and <u>as a group</u> recite the 'Pledge Of Allegiance'.
- <u>Everyone</u> must go across some monkey bars making Tarzan noises.
- Find a juke box, play a popular song and have <u>everyone</u> sing along with it.

Bonus Items: Video Tape The Following—10 points each

- Orange Vehicle
- Pregnant Woman
- Someone dressed in a Halloween outfit. (Not a team member).
- Emergency vehicle
- A Black Cat
- A Scarecrow
- A Spider
- A Volkswagen
- Christmas decorations

IDEA #76

Pass The Spider Race *The idea of passing a spider through their clothes will give most of your guests the creeps.*

Suggested Age: Kindergarten—Adult

Object Of The Game: To be the first team to be tied together by the spider's web.

> ## Supply List
>
> Each <u>team</u> will need:
> 1—20 to 40 foot long piece of **Black Yarn**
> 1 large **Plastic Spider**
>
> **Scissors**

Advance Preparations:

▶ Estimate how long the pieces of yarn should be. They must be long enough to go through both sleeves of each person on the team. This will vary depending on the number of members you will have on each team. It's always safe to over estimate.

▶ Cut the yarn.

▶ Tie one end of each piece of yarn securely to a plastic spider.

▶ Beginning with the end without the spider, roll the yarn into a small ball.

How To Play:

1. Divide your guests into two or more groups and have them stand in a straight line.
2. Explain the object of the game. Demonstrate how each person will need to pass the spider up one sleeve, across their chest, and out the other sleeve.
3. Place the ball of yarn on the ground next to the first person in each line and hand them the spider.
4. On the signal "GO", the first person on each team will pass the spider up one sleeve, across their chest, down their other sleeve, and out to the next person, pulling the string along as they go.
5. The first team to be tied together wins.

SPOOKTACULAR QUIET GAMES

As your guests arrive, you might want to have copies of the *Creepy Word Search* or *Spooky Word Scramble* available for them to work on. Other games that will keep your guests occupied include *Stick The Nose On The Pumpkin*, *Bobbing For Apples*, the *Spooky Feel It Game* and the *Eyeball Toss*.

If you do not have a lot of room to play games, have your guests sit together and play a few rounds of *Halloween Bingo* or *Skeleton Hang Man*. Prior to the party, you can ask each of your guests to bring an inexpensive wrapped Halloween item that can be used as prizes for these games. It will be a lot of fun and your guests will enjoy contributing to the party.

IDEA #77

Stick The Nose On The Pumpkin *Young children love to play this Halloween version of Pin-The-Tail On The Donkey.*

Suggested Age: Preschool—2nd Grade

Object Of The Game: To be the player who sticks the paper nose closest to where it should be on the pumpkin.

Supply List

1 sheet of **Orange Poster Board**	Scissors
1 sheet of **Black Construction Paper**	Glue
Black Felt Tip Marker	Tape
White Crayons	Blindfold

Advance Preparations:

▶ With the black marker, draw a pumpkin on the orange poster board. Cut out the pumpkin.

▶ Using the black construction paper, cut out two eyes and a mouth. Glue onto the pumpkin.

▶ With the remaining black construction paper, cut out a triangle shaped nose for each child.

How To Play:

1. Pass out one triangle to each child. With a white crayon, have them write their name on the triangle.
2. Tape the pumpkin to the wall so it is within reach of the children.
3. Have the children gather in front of the pumpkin and sit down.
4. Explain the object of the game. One important rule is that each player must stick their pumpkin nose to the first place it touches.
5. One player at a time, place a rolled piece of tape on the back of their paper nose and place the blindfold over their eyes. Hand them their nose and slowly spin them around. "Go!"
6. Play continues until each child has had a turn.

IDEA #78

Bobbing For Apples *This old time favorite is still a hit at any Halloween party. If possible, play this game outdoors or in a garage. It can create puddles!*

Suggested Age: Kindergarten—Adult

Object Of The Game: To get an apple out of the water with your mouth while your hands are behind your back.

Supply List

1 **Large Tub** (at least 6" deep)	**Large Pitchers**
Apples—1 for each guest	**Towels**
Water	**Tarp**

Advance Preparations:

► Thoroughly clean the large tub.
► Wash the apples.

On the day of the party:

► Layout the tarp and put the large tub on it.
► Using the large pitchers, fill the tub with at least six inches of water. **Note:** If less water is used your guests will simply pin the apples on the bottom of the tub.
► Place the apples in the water.
► Have the towels available to wipe your guest's wet faces and hair.

How To Play:

1. One guest at a time will kneel down next to the tub and place their hands behind their back.
2. Next, they will plunge their face into the water and try to grab an apple with their teeth. Their hands must stay behind their backs at all times.
3. Allow each guest to have at least four chances to grab an apple.

IDEA #79

Spooky Feel It Game *It is fun to watch the different reactions that the children have while playing this game. Some will want to dig in, while others will be hesitant to play.*

Suggested Age: Kindergarten—5th Grade

Object Of The Game: As you put your hand into each paper sack, guess which part of the monster's body you are feeling.

Supply List

Dried Pears (ears)	7 **Paper Sacks**
Chicken Thigh Bone (fingers)	7 small **Bowls**
Cooked Spaghetti (veins)	7 **Index Cards**
Peeled Grapes (eyes)	**Felt Tip Marker**
Corn Kernels (teeth)	**Yarn**
Corn Silk (hair)	**Scissors**
Banana (tongue)	**Tape**
Hand Towels	**Sandwich Bags**

Advance Preparations:

▶ On each index card write "Guess Which Part?".

▶ Holding the top edge of each index card down, flip up and write what part of the monster they will be feeling. The cards should be labeled as follows: Ears, Eyes, Fingers, Hair, Veins, Teeth, Tongue.

▶ Prepare the 'body parts' and place in individual plastic bags in order to keep them fresh.

On the day of the party:

▶ **Set up as follows:**

• Remove the 'body parts' from the bags and place in the small bowls.

• Unfold the paper sacks and lay them on their sides with the open end facing toward you. Place the bowls inside of the sacks.

- Gather the tops of the paper sacks and tie the yarn or ribbon around them. Make sure you leave an opening that is just barely big enough for the children to get their hands through. You do not want them to see what they are touching.
- Put the appropriate "Guess Which Part?" card along the right hand side of each sack. With the "Guess Which Part?" side of each card up, put a piece of tape along the top edge and tape it securely to the table top. When the cards are flipped up, the children will be able to read which part of the Monster's body they are feeling.
- Place towels next to the messy 'body part' sacks.
- A few adult helpers will need to stand behind the table and help the children as they put their hands in the bags. Younger children may also need help reading the "Guess Which Part?" cards.

How To Play:

1. Tell the children: "Unfortunately we were not able to get a live monster for our Halloween Party. However, we were able to borrow certain parts of it's body from the Mad Scientist. Now it is up to you to guess which parts we were able to get."
2. Tell the children that they will take turns putting their hand in each sack and guessing which part of the Monster's body they are 'feeling'. After they have guessed, flip up the card next to each sack to see if they are right.
3. No peeking is allowed, only touching!

Did You Know?

Frankenstein is a famous horror novel written by Mary Wollstonecraft Shelley in 1818. The book tells the story of a monster that was created by a scientist named Count Frankenstein. The monster has no name in the book.

IDEA #80

Halloween Bingo *This is a game that people of all ages enjoy playing. There are so many variations of this game, they never seem to get tired of it.*

Suggested Age: 2nd Grade—Adult

Object Of The Game: To get BINGO.

Supply List

1 **Bingo Game**
Halloween **M&M's**® (orange and black)
Small **Paper Cups**—1 for each guest
Wrapped Prizes or **Treats**

Advance Preparations:
On the day of the party:
▶ Pour the M&M's® into the paper cups. These will serve as the pieces your guests will use to cover up their numbers.
▶ Set the prizes out on the table so your guests can see what they might win.

How To Play:
1. Give each guest a Bingo card and a cup filled with M&M's®.
2. Tell them what type of Bingo they will be playing and that the M&M's® are to be used as markers on their cards. **DO NOT** eat the M&M's® now, save them until the game is finished.
3. Call out the numbers until one guest calls "BINGO!". Check to make sure they are correct and let them choose a prize.
4. Continue playing until all of the prizes are gone.

Different Types Of "BINGO":
• **Straight Bingo**—Any 5 numbers in a row.
• **B's & O's Bingo**—Fill in the B row *and* the O row only.
• **X Bingo**—Fill in the card like the letter X.
• **Plus Bingo**—Fill in the card like a + sign.
• **Frame Bingo**—Fill in the card like a picture frame.
• **Black Out Bingo**—The whole card must be filled in.

IDEA #81

Guessing Game *It is a lot of fun to see the wide range of guesses that you will get when playing this simple game.*

Suggested Age: 1st Grade—Adult

Object Of The Game: To be the person who has guessed the closest to the correct number of pieces of candy in the jar.

> ## Supply List
> 1 clear **Jar** or **Container**
> **Candy Corn** or **Other Candy**
> **Halloween Wrapping Paper**
> **Shoe Box** with lid
> **Paper**
> **Pencils**
> _____
> **Scissors, Tape**

Advance Preparations:
► Cut the paper into pieces that are large enough for each guest to write their name and their guess on.
► Cut a slit in the top of the shoe box that is large enough for the paper to fit through.
► Wrap the shoe box and lid in Halloween wrapping paper. Make sure the slit in the lid is open.
► Count the candy as you put it in the clear jar or container.
► Write this number on a piece of paper.

How To Play:
1. Give each guest a piece of paper and tell them to write their name and a guess as to how many pieces of candy they think is in the jar.
2. When they are done, have them place their guess in the shoe box.
3. After all of the guesses have been placed in the box, award the jar of candy to the person who has guessed the closest.

Variation:
• Instead of candy, have your guests guess the weight of a pumpkin. The person with the closest guess wins the pumpkin.

IDEA #82

Halloween Candy Drop *If your goblins are getting too excited, calm them down by playing this easy game.*

Suggested Age: Kindergarten—7th Grade

Object Of The Game: To be the first person to get all of the candy into the cup.

Supply List

Each <u>child</u> will need:
- 1– small **Paper Cup**
- 1– **Straw**
- 20 pieces of Halloween **M&M's**® (orange and black)
- 1—zip-top **Plastic Bag**

Advance Preparations:
▶ Place one paper cup, one straw and 20 pieces of candy in each zip-top plastic bag. Each child will get a bag.

How To Play:
1. Give each child one bag.
2. Have the children empty the contents of their bag onto the table.
3. Instruct the children to place the straws on top of a piece of candy, suck in through the straw, pick up the piece of candy and place it in their cup. They may **NOT** use their hands, only their straws.
4. Allow them to practice this skill a few times before starting the game.
5. On the signal "GO", the children will race to see who can get all of their candy into their cup first.

Suggestions:
• Younger children will have trouble sucking through a long straw. Cut the straws in half if young children will be playing this game.

IDEA #83

Eyeball Toss *Have the children make their own Bouncing Eyeballs (page 116) to use in this game.*

Suggested Age: Preschool—5th Grade

Object Of The Game: To score as many points as possible.

> ## Supply List
>
> 5 plastic **Pumpkin Containers**
> 5 **Bouncing Eyeballs** (pg. 116)
> 1 sheet of **Orange Construction Paper**
>
> **Black Marker, Scissors, Masking Tape**

Advance Preparations:

▶ Make at least 5 of the Bouncing Eyeballs on page 116, or purchase balls that look like eyeballs at your local novelty store.

▶ Cut the construction paper into the shape of 5 mini pumpkins.

▶ With the black marker write the numbers 5, 10, 15, 20, and 25 on the mini pumpkins.

On the day of the party:

▶ Make a starting line on the floor with a long piece of tape.

▶ Place the first plastic pumpkin 2 feet in front of the starting line. Just to the right of it, tape the mini pumpkin with the number 5 on it to the floor. Measure 2 more feet and place the second plastic pumpkin and the number 10 mini pumpkin in that area. Continue until you have placed all of the pumpkins in the same manner. **Note:** Depending on the ages of the children, you might have to adjust the distance between the pumpkins.

How To Play:

1. Tell the children to form a straight line behind the starting line.
2. Explain the object of the game and demonstrate.
3. Have the children take turns trying to throw an eyeball into the pumpkins. Each child will get 5 attempts.
4. The child with the highest score wins.

IDEA #84

Skeleton Hang Man *This gives*
a fun Halloween twist to the popular game of Hang Man.

Suggested Age: 2nd Grade—6th Grade

Object Of The Game: To try and guess the Halloween phrase before the skeleton disappears.

Supply List

1 cardboard **Skeleton**	**Paper Fasteners**
2 sheets of **Poster Board**	**Black Marker**

Scissors, Paper Hole Punch, String, Tack

Advance Preparations:

▶ Cut the skeleton into body part sections.
▶ With the paper punch, poke holes in the two adjoining bones and put back together with the paper fasteners.
▶ Cut the poster board into 4 pieces.
▶ Think of a Halloween phrase and make dashes(-) on the piece of poster board for each letter that is in the phrase. For example, the phrase 'Ghosts Live In Haunted Houses' will look like:

- - - - - -   - - - -   - -   - - - - - - -   - - - - - -

▶ Write a different phrase on each piece of poster board. Write the phrase in small letters on the back of each piece of poster board so you don't forget it.

How To Play:

1. Hang the skeleton from the top of a door with the string and tack.
2. Have the children sit on the floor in front of the skeleton.
3. Pick a child to guess a letter that they think is in the phrase. If they guess correctly, write that letter in the correct place(s). If they are incorrect, take away one of the skeleton's bones and write that letter below the phrase in order to keep track of the letters already guessed.
4. The children will take turns guessing until they either guess the phrase or the skeleton runs out of bones.

IDEA #85

Halloween Word Hunt This

is another quiet game that children will find to be fun, yet challenging.

Suggested Age: 3rd—7th Grade

Object Of The Game: To be the person who can make the most words using only the letters in the phrase '**Hallowen Party**'.

Supply List
Each <u>child</u> will need:
1 piece of **Paper**
1 **Pencil**

Advance Preparations:
▶ Decide how the game will be played (see below).
▶ Write the words '**Halloween Party**' at the top of each piece of paper.

Different Ways To Play:

Play individually: Have each child play alone.

Play as a team: Have each child pick a partner and work together on the game.

Play with points: The children will be given 1 point for each letter they use in a word. The longer the word the more points they receive. Bonus points can be given for words found by only one person.

How To Play:
1. Pass out one piece of paper and a pencil to each child.
2. Explain the object of the game and how it will be played.
3. On the signal "GO", the children will begin to find as many words as possible in the phrase '**Halloween Party**'.
4. After a predetermined amount of time (5 to 10 minutes is usually enough), have the children trade papers and as a group, go over the words that were found.

IDEA #86

Spooky Word Scramble

When you need a quieter game, consider playing this one.

Suggested Age: 3rd—7th Grade

Object Of The Game: To be the first team or individual to unscramble all of the words.

> ## Supply List
> Each <u>child</u> will need:
> 1 **Word Puzzle**
> 1 **Pencil**

Advance Preparations:
► Make photocopies of the word puzzle on the following page.
► Decide how the game will be played.

Ways To Play:

Play individually: Each child will do their own puzzle.

Play as a team: Have each child pick a partner and work together on the puzzle.

Race the clock: See who can unscramble the most words in a specific amount of time.

How To Play:
1. Give each child a pencil and a word puzzle.
2. Make sure the word puzzle is turned face down on the table.
3. On the signal "GO", the children can begin unscrambling the words.
4. Play continues until one child or team has unscrambled all of the words. Give some extra time to the children that want to complete their puzzle.
5. Go over the following correct answers: ghosts, Dracula, spider, Frankenstein, skeleton, tombstone, jack-o-lantern, witches, vampire, zombies, goblins, werewolf.

SOTGSH

LRCADUA

RIPDSE

IKSANFEENRTN

LKEOSNTE

TSEMBOTNO

LENA-KJN-RCTOA

SCIHWET

IPEVMAR

MEZBISO

SOGBNIL

ORLEWFEW

Creepy Word Search Children

of all ages enjoy Search and Find Puzzles. The following puzzle has ten different Halloween words for your guests to find.

Suggested Age: 1st Grade—Adult

Object Of The Game: To be the first team or individual to find all of the Halloween words in the puzzle.

Supply List

1—**Puzzle Page** for each guest
1—**Pencil** for each guest

Advance Preparations:

▶ Decide how the game will be played (see below).
▶ Modify the puzzle for the game you have chosen.
▶ Make photocopies of the word puzzle on the following page.

Different Ways To Play:

Young Children:
Highlight or circle the first letter in each word.

Older Children and Adults:
Do not give them the list of words.

Play As A Team:
Have each guest choose a partner and work together on the puzzle.

Race The Clock:
See who can find the most words in a specific amount of time.

HALLOWEEN WORD SEARCH

T	E	B	V	J	I	S	T	I	H
A	O	M	A	B	E	K	L	A	A
E	P	D	M	R	S	E	L	C	U
R	U	A	P	S	M	L	L	I	N
T	M	R	I	H	O	E	U	M	T
R	P	A	R	W	I	T	C	H	E
O	K	R	E	C	E	O	D	L	D
K	I	E	K	O	P	N	G	C	H
C	N	C	M	U	M	M	Y	B	O
I	S	B	N	U	F	L	B	A	U
R	D	I	O	R	E	D	I	P	S
T	L	G	H	O	S	T	N	I	E

HALLOWEEN   VAMPIRE
GHOST   SPIDER
TRICK-OR-TREAT   PUMPKIN
HAUNTED HOUSE   MUMMY
WITCH   SKELETON

Answers To The

HALLOWEEN WORD SEARCH

T			V			S			H
A			A			K		A	A
E	P		M			E	L		U
R	U		P			L			N
T	M		I		O	E			T
R	P		R	W	I	T	C	H	E
O	K		E			O			D
K	I	E				N			H
C	N		M	U	M	M	Y		O
I									U
R			R	E	D	I	P	S	
T		G	H	O	S	T			E

HALLOWEEN   VAMPIRE
GHOST   SPIDER
TRICK-OR-TREAT   PUMPKIN
HAUNTED HOUSE   MUMMY
WITCH   SKELETON

SPOOKTACULAR PARTY FAVORS & CRAFTS

With all of the sweet treats children receive on Halloween, try a different approach to the usual take-home bag of candy. Why not replace it with a 'make and take' craft project? Most are simple, easy-to-make and require materials that are readily available. These craft projects will encourage little ghosts and goblins to be creative and use their imaginations. Most of all, they will have a great time!

IDEA #88

Bouncing Eye Balls *Ghosts*

and goblins of all ages will enjoy making these easy take-home party favors. These bouncing balls can also be used to play the Eyeball Toss game on page 107.

Supply List

Ping-Pong Balls
Black and **Blue Fine Point Permanent Markers**
Red Ultra Fine Point Permanent Markers
1/4" to 1" **Round Lids** or something round to trace around
Pencil

Advance Preparations:

▶ With the pencil, draw an eyeball on each ping-pong ball by tracing around the lids. Use one of the designs in the above picture, or create your own.

How To Make Them:

1. Give each child a ping-pong ball and a marker.
2. With the markers, have the children color the 'pupil' either blue or black. Tell them to use the red marker to draw the 'blood shots' on their eyeballs.

Did You Know?

The only mammals that can fly are bats. While most bats are useful to mankind because they eat vast numbers of harmful insects, the Vampire bat lives on the blood of other animals.

IDEA #89

Ghost Suckers *This easy craft project turns a simple sucker into a ghostly Halloween treat.*

Supply List

For each ghost you will need:
1 **Sucker**
2 8"x8" squares of **White Tissue Paper**
1—10" piece of **Orange Yarn**

—

Black Felt Tip Markers, Scissors

Advance Preparations:
▶ Cut the white tissue paper into 8"x 8" squares.
▶ Cut the yarn into 10" lengths.

How To Make Them:
1. Give each child one sucker, two squares of tissue paper and one piece of yarn.
2. Have the children hold their suckers upright and place the tissue paper over the top of them. The sucker should be placed in the center of the tissue paper.
3. Simply wrap the tissue paper around the sucker.
4. Wrap the yarn around the tissue paper just below the candy ball. Secure with a bow.
5. With the black felt tip markers, have the children draw two eyes and a mouth on their ghostly creations.

Helpful Hint
Large round suckers such as Tootsie Pops® or Blow Pops® work best for this project.

IDEA #90

Paper Sack Pumpkins With

a little creativity, children can turn an ordinary orange paper sack into a Jack-O-Lantern masterpiece.

Supply List

For each Pumpkin you will need:
  1 **Orange Paper Sack**
  18" of **Green Yarn**
  Newspapers—a few pages

**Black Permanent Markers,
Green Acrylic Paint, Paint
Brush, Scissors**

Advance Preparations:
▶ Cut the green yarn into 18" lengths.
▶ With the paper sacks lying flat, paint the top 1/3 of each orange sack green. This will be the pumpkin's stem. Make sure that you get a good coat of green paint on all 4 sides of each paper sack.

How To Make Them:
1. Give each child one paper sack, one piece of yarn and some newspaper.
2. Have the children draw a face on the front of their paper sack.
3. To stuff their pumpkins, have them crumble their newspapers and stuff them inside of the sack.
4. The final step is to twist the green part of the sack to form a stem. Wrap the green yarn around the bottom of the twisted stem and secure with a knot or bow.

Helpful Hint
If you are unable to find orange paper sacks, paint brown or white lunch bags with orange acrylic paint.

IDEA #91

Fuzzy Spiders *Don't be afraid to decorate the corners of your home with these soft spiders.*

Supply List

For each Spider you will need:
- 1-1½" **Black Pom-Pom**
- 2½ **Black Pipe Cleaners**
- 2—7mm **Wiggly Eyes**

Glue, Scissors or **Wire Cutters, Marker, Large Piece Of Paper**

Advance Preparations:

▶ Using scissors or wire cutters, cut the pipe cleaners in half. Each child will need 5 pieces.

▶ On a large piece of paper, copy the spider leg example in Figure 9 .

▶ Make a spider sample by following the directions below. To help bend the legs, refer to Figure 9. The most difficult part of this project is bending the legs.

How To Make Them:

1. Give each child 5 pipe cleaners, 1 pom-pom and 2 wiggly eyes.
2. Using the spider leg example that you have copied, show the children how to bend four of the pipe cleaners into 'legs' just like the drawing.
3. Twist the remaining pipe cleaner around the middle of the 4 'legs' to hold them together. Spread this pipe cleaner to form the last set of 'legs'.
4. Glue the pom-pom on top of the legs.
5. Glue the eyes to the pom-pom.

Figure 9: Spider leg example.

IDEA #92

Ghostly Stick-Ons *These easy-to-make ghosts make fun Halloween gifts for family and friends.*

Supply List

For <u>each</u> ghost you will need:
 4" x 4½" piece of **White Craft Foam**
 1" strip of **Magnetic Tape**
 Scissors
 Black Permanent Markers

Cardboard, Tracing Paper, Pencil, Scissors

Advance Preparations:

▶ With the tracing paper, copy the ghost pattern in Figure 10 onto the cardboard and cut out.

▶ Cut the white craft foam into 4" x 4½" pieces. You should be able to make 12 ghosts out of one 12"x 18" sheet of craft foam.

▶ Cut the magnetic tape into 1" pieces.

▶ Using the cardboard ghost as a pattern, trace the outline of the ghost onto each piece of craft foam with a pencil.

How To Make Them:

1. Give each child one piece of craft foam and one piece of magnetic tape.

2. With their scissors, have the children cut out the ghost by following the drawn lines.

3. With the black markers, have each child draw a face on the ghost. They can copy the design in Figure 10, or create their own.

4. Finally, have them peel the back off of the magnetic strip and stick it onto the back of their ghosts.

Figure 10: Ghost pattern.

IDEA #93

Bare Bones Skeletons *These*

fun-to-make skeletons can be wrapped around almost any-thing: pencils, cabinet or refrigerator doors, on the back of chairs, etc.

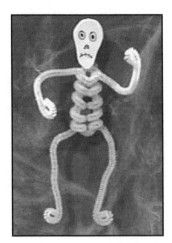

Supply List

For each skeleton you will need:
- 3 **White Pipe Cleaners**
- 1 **Pencil**
- 1"x1½" piece of **White Craft Foam**
- **Black Fine Tip Permanent Markers**

Cardboard, Tracing Paper, Pencil, Scissors, Hot Glue Gun

Advance Preparations:

▶ Using the tracing paper, copy the outline of the skeleton's head in Figure 11a and cut out. Copy this pattern onto the piece of cardboard and cut out.

▶ Cut the craft foam into 1"x1½" rectangles. Using the cardboard head as a pattern, trace the skeleton's head onto each piece of craft foam.

▶ Make at least one sample skeleton.

Suggestion:

• Twisting and putting together the pipe cleaners for this craft can be tricky. It is suggested that you demonstrate the following steps in front of the children, one step at a time, while the children follow along.

Did You Know?
Pipe cleaners are also called chenille stems.

How To Make Them:

1. Give each child three pipe cleaners and one piece of craft foam. They will also need a pencil and scissors.
2. To make the left side of the skeleton's body:
   a. Bend a pipe cleaner into an L shape beginning one inch below one end.
   b. Wrap the pipe cleaner <u>clockwise</u> around a pencil 5 times.
   c. Shape the leg by bending the pipe cleaner as shown in Figure 11b.
3. Make the other half of the body the same way, only wrap the pipe cleaner around the pencil **counter clockwise**.
4. To put the body halves together:
   a. Feed the remaining pipe cleaner through the middle of one set of ribs. See Figure 11c.
   b. Bend the pipe cleaner in half and feed back through the other set of ribs.
   c. Twist both ends around the two neck pieces.
5. Bend the ends of remaining pipe cleaners into hands and feet.
6. With their scissors, have the children cut along the drawn lines on their piece of white craft foam.
7. After cutting, have them draw a scary face on their skeleton's head with a black fine tip marker.
8. Complete the skeletons by having an **ADULT** glue the head onto the neck with the hot glue gun.

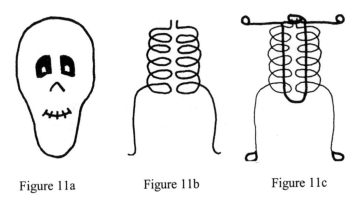

Figure 11a   Figure 11b   Figure 11c

Figure 11: How to assemble the skeleton.

IDEA #94

Ghostly Wind Sock *Hang this ghost outside of your house to greet Trick-Or-Treaters.*

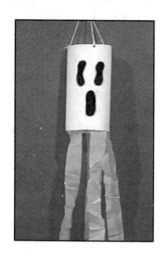

Supply List

For each ghost you will need:
- 1- 11"x 14" piece of **White Poster Board**
- 3 feet of **White Yarn**
- 8 feet of **White Crepe Paper Streamers**

Glue, Black Markers or **Crayons, Scissors, Stapler, Hole Punch**

Advance Preparations:

▶ Cut the poster board into 11"x14" pieces. You should be able to make two ghosts out of one piece of poster board.

▶ On the long side of each piece of poster board, punch three holes approximately 3½ inches apart.

▶ Cut the streamers into 24" lengths. Each child will need 4 streamers.

▶ Cut the yarn into 12" lengths. Each child will need 3 pieces of yarn.

How To Make Them:

1. Give each child a piece of poster board, 4 streamers and 3 pieces of yarn. They will also need glue and a black marker or crayon.
2. Have the children turn the poster board so the holes are at the top.
3. With the black markers or crayons, have them draw the ghost's eyes and mouth in the center of the poster board.
4. Next, have the children glue or staple their 4 streamers along the bottom inside edge of their ghost.

5. Roll the poster board into a tube (face pointing out) and staple shut.
6. To hang their ghosts, have the children tie one end of each piece of yarn through each hole at the top of their ghost.
7. Gather the remaining ends and tie them together.

Variations:
- To make a ghost wind sock that can withstand the weather, use the following materials:

Supply List

For <u>each</u> ghost you will need:
   1 sheet of **White Craft Foam**
   3 feet of **Heavy White String**
   White Plastic Trash Bags
     cut into 4" strips
   Black Permanent Markers

Scissors, Stapler, Hole Punch

Did You Know?

Spiders vary greatly in size. The Comb-Footed Spider is less than 1/50 of an inch long, and are among the world's smallest spiders. The South American Tarantulas are the world's largest spiders. One tarantula measured 10 inches long with its legs extended.

IDEA #95

Slime
You do not have to be a mad scientist to make this ghoulish substance. Simply combine two special potions and you will create Slime.

Supply List

White Glue
Baby Powder
Borax Powder
Water
Green Food Coloring
Plastic Spoons
Mixing Bowls
Funnel
Measuring Cups
Measuring Spoons
2—1 liter **Plastic Bottles**
Zip-Top Plastic Bags

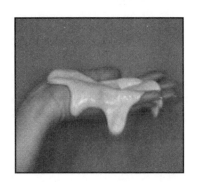

Advance Preparations:

▶ With the funnel, pour the following ingredients into each plastic bottle:

Potion #1: ½ cup baby powder
2½ cups white glue
2 cups water
Green food coloring (add until it's **<u>light</u>** green)

Potion #2: 2 tablespoons borax powder
2 cups warm water

▶ Label the bottles Potion #1 and Potion #2.

On the day of the party:

▶ Set up an area where the children will make the slime. If possible, set up near a sink.

▶ Cover the 'slime area' with newspaper or paper towels for easy clean up. Since the children will get their hands dirty, (that is the fun part) have baby wipes available to clean their hands if a sink is not available.

How To Make It:

1. Divide the children into small groups.
2. At the 'slime area', the children will be given a mixing bowl and spoon.
3. Pour 1/4 cup of Potion #1 into each bowl.
4. With their spoons, they will add 2 to 3 teaspoons of Potion #2 to Potion #1. Stir after each spoonful. By the time the third spoonful has been added, the liquid should change into a dough like substance.
5. Instruct the children to pick up the mixture and knead it with their hands until the liquid is absorbed and is no longer sticky. They can now play with it just like play dough.
6. Place the Slime in a zip-top plastic bag and have them wash up. Instruct the children to place the Slime in their bags after each use. It will last longer.

Helpful Hints:

• Mixing the two potions together is not an exact science. The secret is to add Potion #2 **slowly** to Potion #1, making sure to stir them together as you are pouring. If the mixture becomes hard, not slimy, you have added too much of Potion #2. Throw it away and start over.

• When coloring your Slime, use only a **few** drops of food coloring. Too much food coloring will discolor the children's hands.

• Tell the children to refrigerate their Slime to help keep it fresh. Slime usually lasts between 7 to 10 days, depending upon use.

IDEA #96

Halloween Sugar Art *This colorful project will be a definite Halloween hit!*

Supply List

Baby Food Jars with **Lids**
Orange <u>and</u> **Black Powder**
    Food Coloring
Black Permanent Marker
Sugar

_____

Large Zip-Top Plastic Bags,
2 Large Bowls, Craft Sticks,
Plastic Spoons, Newspapers

Advance Preparations:

▶ Remove all labels and glue from the baby food jars.
▶ Fill all of the jars with sugar.
▶ Take a few of the jars and pour into a zip-top bag. Add orange powder food coloring to the bag, seal, and shake until well mixed. Add additional food coloring until it is bright orange.
▶ Repeat this process with the black powder food coloring.
▶ Continue to color the remaining sugar.
▶ With the permanent marker, color the lids black.

On the day of the party:

• Cover the table with newspapers where the children will be filling their jars.
• Pour the bags of sugar into two large bowls.
• Place the jars, spoons, and craft sticks near the bowls.

How To Make Them:

1. Have the children take a spoon and layer the sugar, one color on top of the other. As the layers are made, push a craft stick down the inside walls of the jar to create designs.
2. Continue layering the sugar until the jar is **<u>completely</u>** full. This will keep the layers from getting mixed together. Place the lid on the jar.

IDEA #97

Play Dough Pumpkins Let

*your little ghosts and goblins play with their play dough
and then they can turn it into a cute take-home pumpkin.*

Supply List

2 cups of **Orange Play Dough**
Clear Plastic Wrap
Green Curling Ribbon
Black Permanent Markers

**Small Mixing Bowl, Large
Saucepan, Large Spoon,
Scissors**

Advance Preparations:

▶ Cut the green curling ribbon into 12" pieces. You will need one
for each pumpkin.
▶ Cut the plastic wrap into 12" x 12" pieces.
▶ Make 2 cups of play dough using the following recipe:

1½ cups **Water**	2 tsp **Orange Food Coloring**
2 Tbs **Cooking Oil**	2 cups **Flour**
½ cup **Salt**	4 Tbs. **Cream of Tartar**

In a small bowl, combine water, food coloring and oil.
Place flour, salt, and cream of tartar into a large saucepan.
Over medium heat, pour the water mixture into the saucepan, stirring constantly. Cook and stir for 5 minutes, until a ball of dough
forms. Cool the dough for 5 minutes, and then knead it with your
hands until it is smooth.

How To Make Them:

1. Roll a piece of play dough into a round ball.
2. Place the ball into the center of a piece of plastic wrap. Pull the
   corners of the plastic wrap over the top of the play dough.
3. Tie the green ribbon around the gathered plastic wrap just above
   the play dough ball. Curl the ribbon with the scissors.
4. With the black marker, draw a Jack-O-Lantern face on the plastic
   wrap.

IDEA #98

Nut Cup Spiders *Don't be fright-ened. These friendly spiders only want to help decorate your Halloween party table.*

Supply List

For <u>each</u> spider you will need:
- 1— **Black Nut Cup**
- 2— **Red 1/4" Pom-Poms**
- 2—7mm **Wiggly Eyes**
- 4—12" **Pipe Cleaners**

Paper Punch, Glue

Advance Preparations:

► With the paper punch, punch 4 holes on each side of the cup. Leave about 1/4" between each hole.

► Make a spider sample by following the directions below. The most difficult part of this project is bending the legs.

How To Make Them:

1. Give each child one nut cup, 2 red pom-poms, 2 wiggly eyes and 4 pipe cleaners.
2. Have the children hold the pipe cleaners together and twist them together in the middle. These will be the legs.
3. Carefully poke 4 of the legs halfway through 4 of the holes in the nut cup. Be careful not to tear the cup. Poke the other 4 legs through the remaining 4 holes. One leg at a time, pull each leg carefully through its hole. (Help young children with this step.)
4. Using the spider leg example in Figure 12, show the children how to bend each of the pipe cleaners to form 'legs'.
5. Glue the red pom-poms along the front edge of the nut cup.
6. Glue the wiggly eyes onto the pom-poms.

Figure 12: Spider leg example.

IDEA #99

Handy Treats Children of all ages
will enjoy making these edible hands.

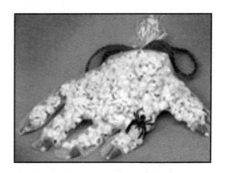

Supply List
Each <u>child</u> will need:
Popcorn
1 clear **Plastic Glove**
5 pieces of **Candy Corn**
12" piece of **Black Yarn**
1 **Spider Ring**
1 small **Plastic Cup**

**Large Bowls with Covers,
Scissors, Ruler**

Advance Preparations:
▶ Pop the popcorn.
▶ Pour the popcorn into the large bowls and cover to keep fresh.
▶ Cut the yarn into 12 inch pieces.

How To Make Them:
1. Give each child a plastic glove, 5 pieces of candy corn, 1 piece of yarn, and a spider ring.
2. Start by putting one piece of candy corn in each finger tip of the glove. If possible, they should try to have the narrow tip of each piece of candy corn pointing out like a fingernail.
3. Using the plastic cups, have them fill their glove with popcorn. They need to make sure the candy corn stays in each of the finger tips while the glove is being filled.
4. Seal the hand by tying the black yarn around the top or 'wrist'.
5. For a final touch, place the spider ring on a finger.

Helpful Hint
If you are short on time, place all items in Step 1 into zip-top bags. Make one for each child and pass them out at the party.

IDEA #100

Black Cat Party Favors

After your little goblin guests make these cats, they can use them to reserve a spot at the dinner table.

Supply List

Black Construction Paper
White Leaded Pencil
Miniature boxes of **Candy**
Glue
Scissors
___
Tracing Paper, Cardboard

Advance Preparations:

▶ Using the tracing paper, copy the outline of the pattern in Figure 13 and cut out. Copy this pattern onto the piece of cardboard and cut out.

▶ Using the cardboard patterns and the white leaded pencil, trace the cat patterns onto the black paper. Make one set for each child.

How To Make Them:

1. Give each child one piece of black construction paper and a box of candy. They will also need glue, scissors and a white leaded pencil.
2. Have the children cut out the cat by following the white lines.
3. Using the white leaded pencil, have each child draw a face on the cat. If you plan to use them as table place cards, have the children write their name below the cat's head.
4. Glue the front and back pieces of the cat to the box of candy.
5. Hold the pieces in place for a minute or two. The cat should now be able to stand alone.

Children enjoy making this easy craft as gifts for family or special friends on Halloween.

Figure 13: Black cat patterns.

IDEA #101

Freaky Beady Spider *Along*
came a spider and sat down beside her ... don't worry, these won't frighten anyone away.

Supply List

For <u>each</u> spider you will need:
  1 yard of **Black Yarn**
  28 - **Black Pony Beads**
  2 - **Yellow Pony Beads**
  2 - **Black Pipe Cleaners**

White Craft Glue, Scissors, Small Bowl

How To Make Them:

1. Cut the yarn into 1 yard pieces.
2. Pour the glue into a small bowl and dip both ends of each piece of yarn into the glue. Let dry.
3. Fold a piece of yarn in half to find the center.
4. String 4 black beads onto the center of the yarn.
5. From the right end, string 5 beads onto the yarn until they are close to the 4 beads. Bend the yarn so the 5 beads are on top of the 4 beads (row 1). See Figure 14.
6. Take the left end of the yarn and thread it through the row of 5 beads (row 2) in the opposite direction of step 5 (left to right). Tighten gently.
7. Continue adding rows of beads in this same manner. Refer to Figure 15 for help.
      Rows 3 <u>and</u> 4 will have 5 black beads,
      Row 5 will have 4 black beads,
      Row 6 will have 2 black beads,
      Row 7 will have 1 yellow, 1 black, 1 yellow bead,
      Row 8 will have 2 black beads.
    Tighten gently after each row.
8. After row 8, tie the yarn in a knot at the top of the head and cut the ends.

9. Cut the black pipe cleaners in half.
10. Thread one pipe cleaner thru row 1.
11. Thread the other pipe cleaners thru rows 2, 4, and 5.
12. Your spider will now have eight legs sticking out. To form the legs, bend them at a 45° angle in the middle and then bend the ends up. See Figure 16.

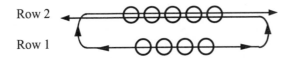

Figure 14: How to string the beads together.

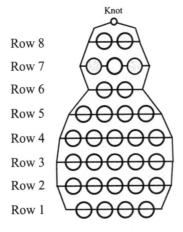

Figure 15: Bead pattern.

Figure 16: How to bend the spider's legs.